Creative Greeting Cards

Sandi
Genovese

Sterling Publishing Co., Inc. New York
A Sterling/Chapelle Book

Chapelle Ltd.

Owner
Jo Packham

Editor
Karmen Quinney

Staff
Ann Bear, Areta Bingham,
Kass Burchett, Marilyn Goff,
Holly Hollingsworth,
Susan Jorgensen, Barbara Milburn,
Linda Orton, Leslie Ridenour, Cindy
Stoeckl, Gina Swapp

Photographer
Kevin Dilley/ Hazen Photography Studio

Library of Congress Cataloging-in-Publication Data

Genovese, Sandi.
   Creative greeting cards / Sandi Genovese.
      p. cm.
   On t.p.: Ellison.
   "A Sterling/Chapelle book."
   Includes index.
   ISBN 0-8069-8779-0
   1. Greeting cards. I Ellison Craft & Design. II. Title.
TT872.G45 2000
745.594'1—dc21   00-037048

10 9 8

First paperback edition published 2001 by
Sterling Publishing Co., Inc.,
387 Park Avenue South, New York, NY 10016
© 2000 by Ellison®
Distributed in Canada by Sterling Publishing
% Canadian Manda Group, 165 Dufferin Street
Toronto, Ontario, Canada M6K 3H6
Distributed in Great Britain by Chrysalis Books Group PLC
The Chrysalis Building, Bramley Road, London W10 6SP, England
Distributed in Australia by Capricorn Link (Australia) Pty. Ltd.
P.O. Box 704, Windsor, NSW 2756 Australia

Printed in China
All Rights Reserved

Sterling ISBN 0-8069-8779-0 Trade
              0-8069-8771-5 Paper

Gotta Have Heart on page 78.

Happy Happy Birthday on page 99.

If you have any questions or comments, please contact: Chapelle Ltd., Inc., P. O. Box 9252 Ogden, UT 84409 (801) 621-2777 ▪ FAX (801) 621-2788 ▪ e-mail: Chapelle@ Chapelleltd.com ▪ website: www.Chapelleltd.com

Sandi Genovese is a multitalented artist, author, and educator, who serves as the creative director at Ellison® Craft & Design, "The Idea Company." She is the diva of die-cuts—developing new ways for teachers and crafters to use Ellison LetterMachine™ and demonstrating her ideas through television appearances, magazine articles, and workshops.

Sandi has written two books on scrapbooking: *Memories in Minutes,* available through Ellison, and *Creative Scrapbooking* from Sterling/Chapelle.

As the senior vice president and creative director for Ellison Craft & Design, Sandi oversees art direction, pioneers new product development, produces videos, writes books and articles, and develops workshops on Ellison products. Sandi still designs new die shapes. In fact, many of the innovations in the industry are the brainchild of Sandi or the Ellison founder, LaDorna Eichenberg.

Sandi Genovese
Senior Vice President and Creative Director,
Ellison® Craft & Design

Sandi travels internationally, giving workshops on greeting cards, scrapbooking, and other craft projects. She has developed ways to use the Ellison LetterMachine beyond paper, such as for rubber stamping, sponge painting, stenciling, and more. She has shown hundreds of thousands of television viewers how to make their projects memorable. Her appearances include Good Morning America, The View, The Carol Duvall Show, Home Matters, and Smart Solutions. She has written numerous articles and created projects for publications such as *Creating Keepsakes, Memory Makers, Good Housekeeping Do It Yourself, Family Circle,* and *Craftrends.*

Special Thanks

I would like to acknowledge and thank my talented creative assistant Kim Fitzgerald and gifted colleagues Cara Mariano and E.L. Smith for their help and support. A special thanks to Liddy Paulsen for turning my handwritten scrawls into legible text, and to Jill Whittaker for initiating this project.

I would also like to thank the following companies and manufacturers for providing materials that were used in this book: Papers from Canson Paper Co.; Daler-Rowney; Keeping Memories Alive; Lasting Impressions; Paper Adventures and Paper Patch; All Night Media; Fiskars Scissors; Marvy Uchida Craft Punches and Pens; McGill Craft Punches; Mrs. Grossman's Stickers; Offray Ribbons; Sakura Pens; and Xyron Adhesives.

Contents

Justin Ames
7 LBS. 6 OZS. 21"
March 25, 1997

General Instructions

Before Starting

As you read this book, it is helpful to understand its basic structure. Each chapter describes a different technique in card creation. The general direction for the techniques is explained in the opening section of each chapter, but not repeated for each example. The specific instructions, materials, and tools needed are listed with each card to make replication of each card quick and easy. Remember the following:

1. Read all General Instructions. Gather all General Materials & Tools along with specific materials and tools for the project.

2. Copy or trace and transfer specific patterns from pages 103–125 onto appropriate card stock or cover stock. Enlarge cards and designs as needed or specified.

3. Cut out cards and designs with craft scissors.

4. Apply glue or desired adhesive to back of designs.

5. Refer to individual project photographs as guidelines for placement of photograph, designs, and stickers.

It is entirely possible to "mix and match" elements from one card to another or to substitute elements more personal to you and the card recipient. Patterns in the back of the book can be enlarged or reduced as desired.

Personalized messages placed on the card can be created with computer-generated fonts and press-on letters, or handwritten with decorative pens. Embellish designs as desired. Details can also be added with stickers, colored pens, and colored pencils.

General Materials & Tools

The following materials and tools are needed to create all the greeting cards in this book. These materials and tools are not listed with the individual projects.

Craft scissors

Glue stick or desired adhesive

Ruler

Tracing paper or photocopy machine for patterns on pages 103–125

Love on page 59.

Adhesives

- **Adhesive Foam Dots** are self-adhesive foam dots about ¼" thick. The adhesive is on both sides. They are used to add dimension to greeting cards. Apply foam dots on the back of photographs and designs to make them literally lift off the card.

- **Double-sided Tape** is a handy alternative to mounting adhesive sheets. It is available in rolls, like regular clear tape, and is applied directly on the back of the cutout or photograph. There are several types of double-sided tape. Some double-sided tape has a peel-off shield to prevent one side from being exposed to dust particles or lint.

- **Foam Tape** is two-sided self-adhesive foam that works the same as the foam dot, but is presented in a roll. Cut segments to the desired size and apply on the back of designs to lift elements off the card.

- **Glue Sticks** are inexpensive and easy to use. Remove the cap, apply the glue directly on the design and adhere the design onto the greeting card.

- **Mounting Adhesive Sheets** are available in 8½" x 11" sheets. Cut a piece of mounting adhesive approximately the same size as the cut-out pattern. Adhere one side of the mounting adhesive onto the back of the

paper and cut out the design. For ease and convenience, a mounting adhesive sheet may be mounted onto an entire sheet of paper before cutting.

- **Sticky Dots** are a sheet of tiny dots that lift off onto the design. Peel off protective liner and place the design onto the sticky dots. Rub your fingers over the shape to transfer the adhesive to the design. Peel liner off and place·design.

- **The Xyron™ Machine** can be used to apply an adhesive on the back of virtually any material. Roll full sheets of paper through the Xyron Machine to apply adhesive. Peel the adhesive backing from the design and place on the greeting card.

Craft Punches

Craft punches generally provide a smaller version of a design for those times when tiny decorations are needed on the greeting card. Both positive and negative shapes may be used. They are available at craft stores and come in a variety of styles, shapes, and sizes.

- **Border Punches** are another type of craft punch. The design is presented in a horizontal strip. When cut from clear plastic, border punches provide an effective tool for making a stencil.

- **Corner Punches** are used for rounding corners of greeting cards and photographs. Some corner rounders punch a decorative element in the corner of the card at the same time.

- **Hand-held Craft Punches** resemble the traditional hand-held hole punch but have a decorative shape instead of a plain round hole.

- **Thumb Punches** use the palm of the hand or the thumb to apply pressure for cutting. Thumb punches are available in small, large, jumbo, and in a wide variety of designs.

A hand-held craft punch was used to create the tiny hearts surrounding the window of this Dangle Card. See page 93.

Patterns

Each greeting card described in this book comes with its own pattern(s) that can be found on pages 103–125. Do not cut out the patterns from this book. Trace patterns onto tracing paper or photocopy, then cut out patterns. Transfer patterns onto desired card stock or cover stock. Cut out designs.

Patterns can also be photocopied at a copy center directly onto card stock. All patterns are actual size unless otherwise noted. Many patterns include perforated lines to use as guidelines for creasing or for embellishing in contrasting colors. Solid lines are used as guidelines for cutting or making slits.

If you do not wish to use the patterns in this book, die-cuts are an option. A list of Ellison dies is provided on page 126, which corresponds with the patterns on pages 103–125.

Die-cuts

Die-cuts are precut shapes of paper or lightweight card stock. Most of the patterns provided in this book are available in die-cuts. They are made by putting a die into a special press called a die-cutting machine, along with the desired paper, card stock, or clear page protector.

They are one of the easiest ways to decorate a greeting card and may be used to replace hand-cut designs. Adhere die-cuts onto cards, using a glue stick, or mount onto the cards with mounting adhesive sheets. It is easiest to mount adhesive to paper first, then cut in a die-cutting machine. Die-cuts are available at most craft stores and are sold individually or in theme packets. All of the card formats are also die-cuts.

Die-cutting machines are available for use in many craft stores. Stores generally do not charge to use the machines, if you purchase the paper or card stock from the store. Also, look for them in stationery stores, fine-art stores, photograph shops, and stores that sell rubber stamps.

Die-cutting machines allow for creative control when cutting shapes and letters for greeting cards. Select your own paper colors and designs for the die-cuts. Cut as many of each design or letter as needed for your greeting cards. Cut a wide assortment of products, such as maps, theater programs, sheet music, comic strips, wallpaper, self-adhesive paper, etc. You can even cut rubber for rubber stamps of your own design. Die-cutting machines will cut anything scissors will cut; fabric, felt, thin plastic, and other decorative elements can be added to your greetings cards. Die-cutting machines can also be used to emboss elegant features on cards.

Embellishments

Transform a simple design into a finely detailed design. See photograph. Embellishing can be as simple as cutting the stem off of a green apple and placing it on a red apple, or placing a gold fish with pierced holes over a green fish.

Embellish a design by adding multiple layers of patterned or contrasting paper for more detail.

Embellish a design by cutting one design from multiple colors. Trim away the unwanted sections and layer on top of base shape.

Lettering and Pens

Lettering can be computer-generated, handwritten, or pressed on using stickers or press-on letters.

- **Black Felt-tipped Pens** are available in varying sized tips and are perfect for drawing line borders on cards and handwriting a message.

- **Colored Felt-tipped Pens** are great for hand-coloring details on a card.

- **Gel Roller Pens** are similar to paint pens but create a finer line. The color is not as saturated, but is easier to work with. Also, there are no problems with paint clumping or skipping.

- **Paint Pens** make it easy to put any color print on top of any color material. The product in the pen is paint and makes a fairly thick line.

Papers

Choices for paper have never been greater. From handmade paper, to paper for scrapbooking, to colorful stationery, paper is available in an endless variety of colors, patterns, textures, and weights. Use these varieties to help create themes and moods.

- **Cover Stock** and **Card Stock** are more rigid than paper, making excellent choices for cards and card covers.

- **Legal Size Papers** are available at office supplies stores. They measure 8" x 14".

- **Page Protectors** are easily cut into various envelope sizes for a special see-through card effect.

- **Plain-colored Papers** are available in a wide range of weights. In most cases, the bulk of the card will be cut from plain and contrasting-colored card stock, with patterned or textured paper for accent pieces.

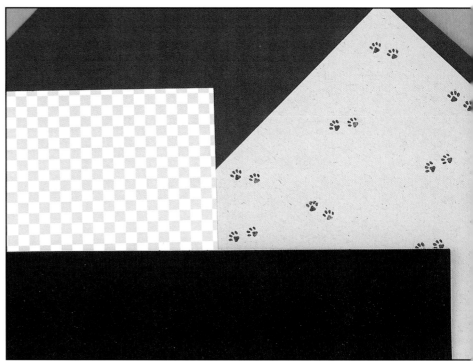

- **Patterned Papers**, such as stationery or wrapping paper, are medium- to lightweight. They add contrast or complement other decorative elements on the card.

- **Vellum Paper** adds a unique feature to cards. The vellum allows elements on the card to be visible through a filmy layer of paper. Print or photocopy directly onto its surface for a very special effect.

Stickers

Stickers add a decorative element to greeting cards. Use elegant stickers to decorate a wedding or anniversary card and whimsical designs for a child's birthday party invitation.

- **Border stickers** are created specifically for use as borders called design lines.

- **Stickers** are available in a wide variety of styles, covering a large assortment of themes.

Paper Cutters, Scissors, and Trimmers

Many craft stores have heavy-duty paper cutters for your use. Some are available with different blades or decorative edges.

- **Decorative-edged Scissors** are used for enhancing the edges and corners of paper motifs, mats, photographs, and card edges. There is a wide variety of edge patterns from simple scallops to lacy Victorian.

- **Decorative Corner Edgers** create a patterned edge for each corner of the card. The pattern can be continued down the four sides of the card, or used solely as a corner design.

- **Paper Trimmers and Scissors** are used for cutting paper, light plastic, and other materials. Select a pair with comfortable handles to make card projects easier. A small pair helps to trim with better control.

Rubber Stamps

Rubber stamps provide another option for decorating greeting cards. They are easy to use and come in a wide variety of shapes and sizes, making it easy to find stamps to coordinate with the theme of a card. Decorate the image with felt-tipped pens after stamping, or emboss them with embossing powder and powder heating tools. It is also possible to make your own patterned paper, using tiny rubber stamps. Ink pads can be used with any traditional rubber stamp and come in every color of the rainbow. There are many stamps available that decoratively print the lines of information for party and shower invitations or birth announcements.

Creative Greeting Cards

A distinctive envelope arrives in the mail among bills, junk mail, and catalogs. The bulk of the mail is discarded while the envelope gathers all of your attention. Why is that? You know that inside is a special offering selected or created with one person in mind . . . you! There is no doubt that a unique card creates a vibrant impression, stronger and more lasting than any phone call, fax, or e-mail.

There are many reasons for creating a special card for a special friend. A handmade card allows for the message to fit the person or occasion in a way that a store-bought card cannot. The card can reflect the personality of the card maker as well as the recipient.

Creating your own cards, makes good sense financially. Store-bought cards can be expensive. Making a card by hand is a great way to save a little money. It also provides an opportunity to use remnants from around the house—everything from wrapping paper to string, from buttons to wallpaper, and more.

The therapeutic value of card creation is priceless. A creative outlet for ideas can be as relaxing as a day at the beach.

Whether you are just beginning your card-making skills or are already a veteran card maker, you will find the creation of these quick and easy. Don't be misled into thinking that these cards are difficult to make. Whether working with die-cut shapes or the patterns provided in the back of the book, the basic card design is complete with perforation lines and cutouts, making replication easier than you might think. Included are cards for all occasions: Christmas, Hanukkah, birthdays, Easter, Halloween, valentines, Mother's Day, Father's Day, wedding, and just to say hello. In addition, you will find birth announcements, party invitations, and thank you cards. Each card is designed to convey a message in a unique and special way.

I hope the cards in this book help to jump-start your creativity and inspire you to create your own clever cards.

Thank You on page 55.

Greeting Card Tips

- Make certain to start with the envelope. Whether your card is being sent through the mail or left under a pillow, the presentation is more special if the card is housed in an envelope. Whether the envelope is purchased or handmade, select it first and create your card to fit.

- Remember the value of a black or white background for your cards. There is nothing that will make bright colors pop like basic black or white.

- Be aware that substitution is always possible. Replace primary colors with pastels. Substitute patterned card stock for plain card stock. Trade star stickers for hearts. Make each project as personal as possible by selecting the products, styles, and themes that are personal favorites of the card maker or the card recipient.

- When planning your card composition, keep in mind that it is good to have an element that slightly overlaps another element. Both elements should be clearly visible, but a slight overlap helps to keep the composition from looking too rigid or too symmetrical.

- Know when to stop. Usually the best design is deceivingly simple and clean. Too much activity in the design will only be confusing and isn't as appealing as a sharp clean look.

- Remember the third dimension. Cards don't have to be limited to a flat surface. Elements can pop up or hang down for a very special effect.

What's Up? on page 36.

- Remember you have the perfect tool right in your photograph album to personalize many cards. Birth announcements, graduation, and annual Christmas cards are only enhanced by the inclusion of a photograph. Instead of tucking the photograph in the envelope, build the photograph into the design of the card. Copy favorite photographs and save your valuable originals. Color copy machines and duplicate photograph machines are readily available and make this a simple task.

- Multiple mats are a quick and easy way to add bright color and detail to any card. A thin line or border drawn with a pen and ruler can enhance a multiple mat.

- Organize supplies and keep them handy, allowing you to grab a few minutes here and there to work on cards.

- Try to set aside a little time on a consistent basis for card creation. If a given time is scheduled, you are more likely to get to it.

- Jot down notes for future cards and store them with your supplies. Note which cards you have sent special friends to avoid sending a similar card in the future.

Accordion Cards

Accordion Cards involve the folding of paper into accordion pleats. The pleats can vary in number and size and can be presented horizontally or vertically. The pleats fold up fairly flat, but will spread when opened to reveal several layers of design in a card.

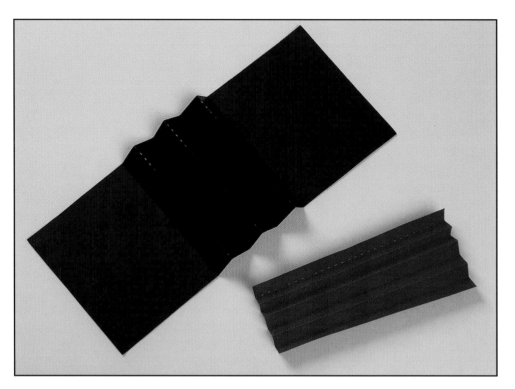

Accordion Cards are created with either an Accordion Card Pattern on page 104, Accordion Fold #1 Pattern on page 103, or Accordion Fold #2 Pattern on page 105. (Accordion Card is on the left and Accordion Fold #1 is on the right in the photograph above.)

The Accordion Card or the Accordion Fold #1 is attached onto front and back card covers. See photograph at left. Accordion Fold #2 is not shown.

Hugs & Kisses

Instructions

Refer to General Instructions on pages 5–13.

1. Enlarge Accordion Fold #2 Pattern 38%. Transfer pattern onto white cover stock.

2. Cut out card.

3. Cut cover ⅛" larger than card all around from black cover stock. Center and adhere card onto cover.

4. Crease card on perforation lines, creating pleats.

5. Cut Xs and Os as desired from assorted colored card stock, varying sizes.

6. Adhere Xs and Os onto inside back of card and pleats, allowing portion of each letter to extend over edges of pleats.

7. Place letters on left-hand side of card for Hugs & Kisses.

8. Cut strip from red cover stock to fit horizontally inside card. Note: The size of strip will be determined by length of message.

9. Using black pen and ruler, draw pen lines onto strip. Write desired message on strip.

10. Adhere strip onto inside of card.

Materials & Tools

Black felt-tipped pen

Card stock: assorted colors; assorted patterns

Cover stock: black; red; white

Pattern: Accordion Fold #2 (pg. 105)

Press-on letters for Hugs & Kisses: ¼"

Ruler

Zing Went the Strings of My Heart

Instructions

Refer to General Instructions on pages 5–13.

1. Enlarge Accordion Fold #2 Pattern 38%. Transfer pattern onto white cover stock.

2. Transfer Primitive Heart Pattern onto patterned card stock. Repeat. Repeat two times with red card stock.

3. Cut out card and designs. Using craft knife, cut two vertical slits into each heart.

4. Weave thread through slits in hearts.

5. Cut cover ¼" larger than card all around from black cover stock. Center and adhere card onto cover.

6. Cut thin strip from black card stock to fit horizontally inside bottom of card.

7. Using silver pen, write desired message on black strip. Adhere strip onto card.

8. Crease card and cover on perforation lines, creating pleats.

9. Adhere hearts onto each panel, overlapping third and fourth heart. See photograph. Place foam dots on back of third heart.

10. Pull thread to allow play when pleats are closed and opened. Trim excess thread.

11. Using black pen, complete message. See photograph.

Materials & Tools

Adhesive foam dots

Black thread

Card stock: black; red; red/white patterned

Cover stock: black; white

Craft knife

Patterns: Accordion Fold #2 (pg. 105); Primitive Heart (pg. 103)

Pen: black felt-tipped; silver metallic

Joy to the World

Instructions

Refer to General Instructions on pages 5–13.

1. Enlarge Accordion Fold #2 Pattern 38%. Transfer pattern onto cover stock.

2. Transfer Hook Pattern onto black card stock. Repeat three times.

3. Transfer Christmas Ornament #1B Pattern onto blue card stock. Repeat three times with assorted colored card stock.

4. Cut out card and designs. Using craft knife, cut out highlights for ornaments. See photograph. Adhere a piece of contrasting colored card stock onto back of highlight on back of ornaments.

5. Crease card on perforation lines.

6. Cut 4½" x 6" rectangle from cover stock. Adhere to last panel.

7. Insert hooks through ornaments.

8. Draw continents on green card stock and cut out. Adhere onto blue ornament. Adhere ornament onto last panel of card.

9. Using red pen, write desired message on last panel inside of card around ornament.

Materials & Tools

Card stock: assorted colors; black; blue; green

Cover stock: white

Craft knife

Patterns: Accordion Fold #2 (pg. 105); Christmas Ornament #1B (pg. 103); Hook (pg. 103)

Red fine-point felt-tipped pen

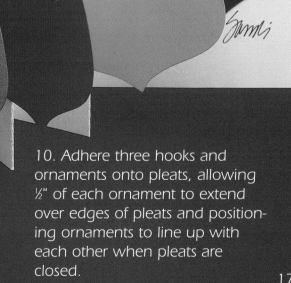

10. Adhere three hooks and ornaments onto pleats, allowing ½" of each ornament to extend over edges of pleats and positioning ornaments to line up with each other when pleats are closed.

For Whom the Bell Jingles

Ask Not
For
Whom
The Bell
Jingles

Materials & Tools

Black felt-tipped pen

Christmas floral sticker

Cover stock: cream; green; red

Double-sided tape

Green ribbon: ⅛"-wide

Jingle bells: small (2); med.

Patterns: Accordion Fold with Slits (pg. 105); Large Accordion Card (pg. 105)

Ruler

Instructions

Refer to General Instructions on pages 5–13.

1. Enlarge Large Accordion Card Pattern 35%. Enlarge Accordion Fold with Slits Pattern 52%.

2. Transfer Large Accordion Card Pattern onto cream cover stock. Cut out card.

3. Cut out 3"-wide rectangle from center of card. Crease card on perforation lines, creating pleats.

4. Transfer Accordion Fold with Slits Pattern onto red cover stock. Cut out Accordion Fold with Slits. Cut slits in fold as shown on pattern. Crease fold on perforation lines, creating pleats.

5. Position red fold in cream card, using slits. See photograph at right.

6. Cut three pieces of ribbon into desired lengths to hang jingle bells from card. Thread one end of ribbon through hook on each jingle bell. Tape ribbon ends onto back of card in pleats.

7. Cut two 4" x 6½" covers from green cover stock for front and back.

8. Adhere one end of card ¼" in from edge of front cover. Repeat for remaining end of card and back cover.

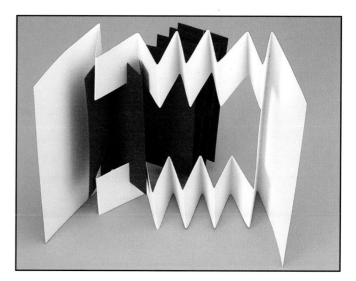

9. Cut two 2¾" x 5½" rectangles from red card stock.

10. Using black pen, write desired message on rectangles. Center and adhere rectangles onto front and back inside of card. See photograph at right.

11. Cut 3" x 5" rectangle from cream cover stock to decorate front cover.

12. Using black pen and ruler, create border around rectangle. Write desired message on rectangle.

13. Center and adhere rectangle onto front of cover. Place floral sticker over top edge of cream rectangle.

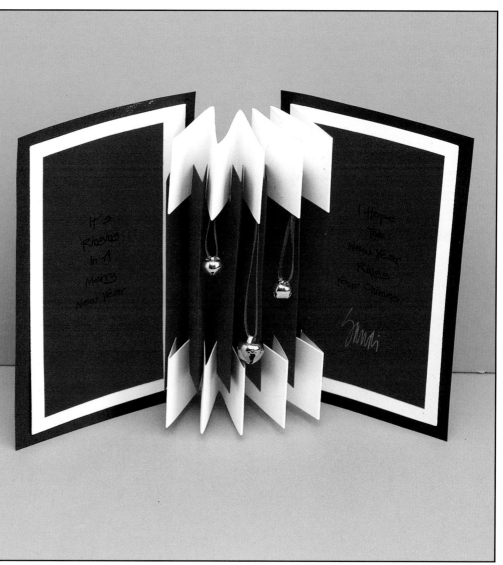

New Year's Card

Materials & Tools

Adhesive foam dots

Black paper

Card stock: black; blue; gold; gold metallic; green; purple; red

Computer

Cover stock: white, 35" x 6½"

Gold metallic pen

Patterns: Christmas Ornament #2A (pg. 104); Current Year (pg. 103); Holly Leaves (pg. 104); Primitive Star (pg. 104); Tiny Christmas Light (pg. 104); Upcoming Year (pg. 103)

Red jingle bell

Ruler

Stickers: border; floral; heart; lips; star

Thumb punch: mini Christmas tree

White thread

Instructions

Refer to General Instructions on pages 5–13.

Note: Designs are all cut in pairs.

1. Fold white cover stock into seven equal panels. See photograph. Note: Each panel measures 5"x 6½".

2. Using craft knife, cut out 2¾" square from center of each panel.

3. Transfer Christmas Ornament #2A Pattern onto gold card stock. Repeat. Cut two.

4. Transfer Holly Leaves Pattern, and Current Year onto green card stock. Cut two of each.

20

5. Transfer Primitive Star Pattern onto red card stock. Cut two.

6. Transfer Tiny Christmas Light Pattern onto purple card stock. Cut two. Repeat with blue card stock. Cut two.

7. Transfer Upcoming Year Pattern onto purple card stock. Cut two. Repeat with metallic card stock. Cut one.

8. Using thumb punch, punch out four trees.

9. Cut seven pieces of thread into desired lengths to hang designs from card. Thread one end of thread through hook on jingle bell. Sandwich double thread vertically between two ornament cutouts.

10. Sandwich one end of thread vertically between each set of cutouts except metallic design. Match and adhere designs together. Using various stickers, hang thread from center front of panels, leaving designs to dangle freely. See photograph on facing page.

11. Print corresponding messages in reverse type with borders to appear under each window. See Card's Mes-sage below. Note:

Black card stock and white felt-tipped pen can be used if a computer is not available or desired. Cut messages into equal-sized strips.

12. Adhere one strip ¼" below each window.

13. Cut 12" x 4" rectangle from red card stock for slider.

14. Wrap slider around card, overlapping short ends in back. Adhere ends.

15. Cut 2½" x 3½" rectangle from black card stock. Center and adhere metallic design onto rectangle as desired.

16. Place two foam dots on back of rectangle. Place rectangle on front of slider as desired.

17. Using gold pen and ruler, create border around outside of rectangle.

Card's Message:

Kiss the Century Good-Bye (first panel)

It's Been Delightful (second panel)

Time for a Shiny New Beginning (third panel)

Think Tree Mendous Thoughts (fourth panel)

Ring in the New Century (fifth panel)

And Have a Happy Holly Day (sixth panel)

Enjoy . . . Burma Shave (seventh panel)

Thought I'd Drop You a Line

Just Thought I'd Drop You a Line

Materials & Tools

Card stock: assorted colors; black/white polka-dot; red

Corner rounder

Cover stock: black; yellow

Patterns: Accordion Card (pg. 104); Clothespin (pg. 103); Tiny Push Pin (pg. 103)

Pens: black felt-tipped; silver metallic

White twine

Instructions

Refer to General Instructions on pages 5–13.

1. Enlarge Accordion Card Pattern 55%. Transfer pattern onto black cover stock.

2. Transfer Tiny Push Pin Pattern onto red card stock.

3. Transfer Clothespin Pattern onto assorted colored card stocks. Repeat eight times.

4. Cut out card and designs.

5. Crease card on perforation lines, creating pleats.

6. Cut 4¼" x 5" covers from yellow card stock for front and back.

7. Using corner rounder, round corners of covers.

8. Cut two 3½" x 4¼" mats from white card stock.

9. Cut 3½" x 2¾" rectangle from polka-dot card stock. Cut mat ⅛" larger than rectangle all around from red card stock.

10. Adhere one end of card ⅛" down from top edge onto white mat. Repeat for remaining end of card and mat.

11. Center and adhere white mat onto front and back cover.

12. Adhere red mat slightly off-center onto front of cover. Center and adhere polka-dot mat onto red mat.

13. Using silver pen, color hinges of clothespins and points of push pins. Adhere one clothespin onto front of cover.

14. Cut 12" piece of twine. Adhere eight clothespins onto pleats, weaving twine among clothespins.

15. Adhere one push pin 1" from each twine end, adhering both twine and push pin onto card.

16. Cut strip from white card stock to fit horizontally inside of card. Note: The size of strip will be determined by length of message.

17. Using black pen, write desired message on strip.

18. Adhere strip onto inside of cover.

Father's Day

When closed, the accordion card appears quite ordinary; but opened, it reveals a forest of colorful designs. Above and below are two other examples for Accordion Cards.

Congratulations

23

Simply Tree Mendous

Materials & Tools

Barnwood patterned paper

Card stock: green; white

Cover stock: burgundy; green, 8½" x 11"

Double-sided tape

Gold metallic pen

Patterns: Accordion Card (pg. 104);
  Country Christmas Tree (pg. 104)

Photograph: 3⅝" x 2⅞"

Press-on letters for Tree Mendous: ¼"

Stickers: Christmas floral; tiny star (2)

Instructions

Refer to General Instructions on
pages 5–13.

1. Enlarge Accordion Card Pattern 55%.
Transfer pattern onto green cover stock.

2. Transfer Country Christmas Tree
Pattern onto white card stock. Repeat
four times.

3. Cut out card and designs.

4. Crease card on perforation lines,
creating pleats.

5. Cut cover ½" larger than front and
back panel of card all around from
burgundy cover stock.

6. Tape one end of card ½" down from
inside top of front cover. Repeat for
remaining end of card and back cover.
See photograph on page 14.

7. Cut tree trunks from barnwood paper. Adhere trunks onto trees. Adhere trees into three pleats as desired.

8. Place letters on inside of card for Tree Mendous message. See photograph at right.

9. Cut mat ⅛" larger than photograph all around from white card stock.

10. Center and adhere photograph onto mat. Center and adhere mat onto inside bottom of card.

11. Cut 4¼" x 3" rectangle from green card stock to decorate front cover.

12. Cut mat ⅛" larger than rectangle all around from white card stock.

13. Using gold pen, write desired message on rectangle.

14. Center and adhere rectangle onto mat. Place tiny star stickers on mat. Adhere mat onto front of cover. Place Christmas sticker on top edge of mat.

Happy Birthday

Decorated with candles and a party noisemaker, this makes the perfect birthday card for any age. Match the numbers of candles to the years old for an especially personal touch.

Pocket Cards

Pocket Cards are perfect for giving items such as money, gift certificates, or theater tickets. These cards have a pocket that sits on the cover. The pocket is adhered to the cover on the sides and bottom, but the top is left open, allowing for the inclusion of any number of special items. Be certain to create your card and envelope large enough to accommodate the size of the item that will be placed in the pocket.

If a pocket is being made for a photograph, start with a pocket large enough to hold the photograph and create the card to fit. Make certain there is an envelope sized to fit as well.

A note can always be folded to fit in a pocket, but this is not the case with a photograph.

Decorated with hearts and a simple "I Love You", this Pocket Card will be a hit with your loved one.

Making Pockets

1. Cut card stock or cover stock approximately ⅓–½ the vertical size of the cover.

2. Using glue stick, apply narrow strip of glue on sides and bottom of card.

3. Adhere pocket onto bottom front of card.

Happy Birthday

Materials & Tools

Card stock: assorted colors;
  assorted patterns; black/white
  polka-dot; gold; red; white

Cover stock: black

Pattern: Candles (pg. 106)

Pen: gold metallic

Instructions

Refer to General Instructions on pages 5–13.

1. Transfer Candles Pattern onto assorted colored and gold card stocks. Cut out candles.

2. Trim flame off of assorted colored candles and adhere onto gold candles.

3. Cut 6¼" x 9¼" card from black cover stock. Fold in half widthwise.

4. See Making Pockets on page 26. Create pocket from polka-dot card stock.

5. Cut mat ⅛" larger than pocket all around from red card stock. Center and adhere pocket onto mat.

6. Adhere 4–5 candles onto pocket, extending candle flame over top of pocket.

7. Adhere bottom and side edges of pocket onto bottom front of card, leaving room for desired item to slide inside.

8. Using gold pen, dot around candle flames.

9. Use remaining candles to decorate inside of card. Using gold pen, write birthday message.

Cute as a Button

Materials & Tools

Card stock: assorted colors; black; white; yellow

Cover stock: white

Pattern: Tiny Button (pg. 107)

Pens: black felt-tipped; silver metallic

Photograph: 3" x 5"

Ruler

Instructions

Refer to General Instructions on pages 5–13.

1. Transfer Tiny Button Pattern onto assorted colored card stocks. Repeat six times.

2. Cut out designs.

3. Cut 6¼" x 9¼" card from white cover stock. Fold in half widthwise.

4. See Making Pockets on page 26. Create pocket from black card stock.

5. Crop photograph as desired. Adhere photograph onto yellow card stock. Trim yellow card stock all around photograph as desired, creating mat. Note: Photograph will be item that is placed into pocket.

6. Adhere buttons onto top pocket edge, overlapping each other.

7. Using silver pen, draw stitch marks around pocket and thread through buttons.

8. Cut 2" x 1" strip from white card stock to fit horizontally on pocket.

9. Using black pen, write desired message on strip. Adhere strip onto bottom front of pocket.

10. Adhere bottom and side edges of pocket onto bottom front of card, leaving room for photograph to slide inside.

11. Use remaining buttons to decorate inside of card. Using black pen, write birth information.

Decorated with bandages, pills, and a stethoscope, this Pocket Card is perfect for someone feeling under the weather. Aspirin, cough drops, or candy placed in the pocket is sure to lift their spirits.

Decorated with a baseball, shirt pocket, and stars, this Pocket Card is for the sports fan in your life. The recipient will especially love the tickets to a favorite sporting event.

Happy Holidays

Materials & Tools

Card stock: gold metallic

Christmas floral sticker

Cover stock: burgundy; cream; green

Gold metallic pen

Pattern: Small Primitive Star (pg. 107)

Ruler

Instructions

Refer to General Instructions on pages 5–13.

1. Transfer Small Primitive Star Pattern onto card stock. Repeat two times.

2. Cut out designs.

3. Cut 6¼" x 9¼" card from green cover stock. Fold in half widthwise.

4. See Making Pockets on page 26. Create pocket from burgundy cover stock.

5. Cut mat ⅛" larger than pocket all around from burgundy cover stock.

6. Cut strip from burgundy cover stock to fit horizontally on pocket. Note: The size of strip will be determined by length of message.

7. Using gold pen and ruler, create border around strip. Write desired message on strip.

8. Adhere strip onto pocket. Place floral sticker on top edge of pocket.

9. Adhere bottom and side edges of pocket onto bottom front of card, leaving room for desired item to slide inside.

10. Adhere stars onto front of card.

11. Using gold pen, dot around stars.

12. Line inside of card with contrasting paper. Using gold pen, write desired message.

Pop-Up Cards

Pop-up Cards involve the cutting and folding of pop-up tabs, which allow the decorative elements inside the card to pop right off the page.

The number, size, and placement of the tabs can vary, depending on the items that will be presented on each tab. A cover is needed to conceal the notches cut in the card that make the pop-up tabs.

The pop-up format can be used for any theme, simply by substituting other designs for the hearts. It is equally effective to decorate each pop-up tab with stickers, photographs, craft punch art, or rubber-stamped designs. In any case, the insides are hidden until the recipient opens the card. The pop-up tabs then spring to life, catching the unsuspecting recipient by surprise.

I Love You

Materials & Tools

Adhesive foam dots

Black felt-tipped pen

Card stock: assorted patterns; black; black/white pin-dot; white

Cover stock: red; white

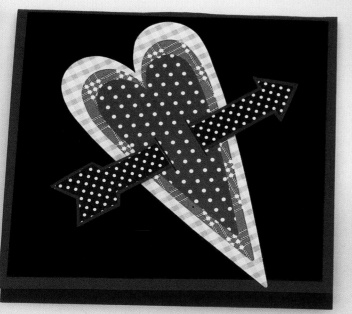

Patterns: Arrow (pg. 106); Lollipop Alphabet (pg. 125); Pop-Up #1 (pg. 106); Pop-Up #3 (pg. 106); Primitive Hearts (pg. 107)

Ruler

Stickers: checkered strips; hearts; polka-dot strips

Instructions

Refer to General Instructions on pages 5–13.

1. Enlarge Pop-Up #1 Pattern 50%. Enlarge Pop-Up #3 Pattern 50%.

2. Transfer Arrow Pattern onto pin-dot card stock.

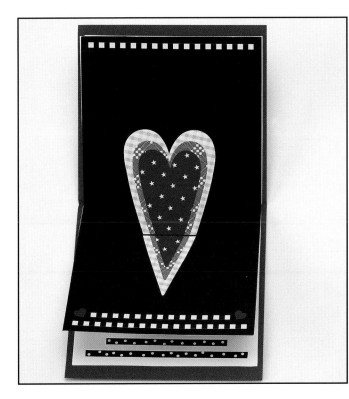

3. Transfer Pop-Up #1 Pattern onto white cover stock, creating card #1. Repeat with black card stock, creating card #2.

4. Transfer Pop-Up #3 Pattern onto white card stock, creating card #3.

5. Transfer Lollipop Alphabet Pattern for i, YOU, and Primitive Hearts Pattern onto patterned card stocks. Repeat for Primitive Hearts. Note: Enlarge letters for i and YOU as desired.

6. Cut out cards, designs, and letters.

7. Crease cards and pop-up tabs on perforation lines.

8. Adhere i onto black card stock. Trim, leaving 1/16" border.

9. Adhere i onto pop-up tab of card #1.

10. Cut dot for i from assorted card stock. Repeat four times, getting successively smaller. Layer and adhere dots together, largest to smallest.

11. Place layered dot on foam dot. Adhere onto inside of card above i. Place polka-dot strip stickers 1/8" from top and bottom on card #1.

12. Layer and adhere three heart designs together, largest to smallest. Repeat for remaining three hearts.

13. Adhere back of one heart set onto pop-up tab of card #2. Crease bottom of heart to match crease at bottom of pop-up card. Cut heart off at crease and adhere below crease of pop-up. See photograph at top left.

14. Place checkered strip stickers 1/8" from top and bottom of card #2.

15. Cut YOU from assorted card stock. Adhere each letter onto black card stock. Cut around each letter, leaving 1/16" border. Note: Leave center of O solid.

16. Adhere heart stickers to O. Adhere bottom back of letters onto pop-up tabs of card #3.

Continued on page 34.

33

Continued from page 33.

17. Place polka-dot strip stickers ⅛" in from top and bottom of card #3.

18. Adhere bottom of first card to top of second card. Adhere bottom of second card to top of third card. Note: This process can be repeated, adding as many pages as desired.

19. Cut 4½" x 8½ cover from red cover stock.

20. Fold cover, creating spine to accommodate thickness of inside pages.

21. Adhere card cover to pop up book, leaving narrow border all around.

22. Cut 4¼" x 4" rectangle from black card stock for front of cover.

23. Adhere remaining layered hearts onto rectangle as desired.

24. Adhere arrow onto red card stock. Trim, leaving 1⁄16" border. Cut arrow in half.

25. Using black pen and ruler, draw lines on center of heart to look like slits.

26. Place one foam dot behind tip of arrow and base of arrow. Match and place front half of arrow onto right slit line. Match and place back half of arrow onto left slit line, leaving open space in middle.

27. Center and adhere black rectangle onto front of cover.

28. Place heart stickers inside of card as desired.

You're Invited

Materials & Tools

Adhesive foam dots

Black felt-tipped pen

Black ink pad

Card stock: assorted colors; green/ white pin-dot; red; white; yellow

Cover stock: black; white

Patterns: Balloons (pg. 109); Noise-maker (pg. 109); Pop-Up #1 (pg. 106); Splash (pg. 109)

Rubber stamp: invitation

Ruler

Instructions

Refer to General Instructions on pages 5–13.

1. Enlarge Pop-Up #1 Pattern 50%. Transfer pattern onto white cover stock.

2. Transfer Balloons Pattern and Noisemaker Pattern onto assorted colored card stock.

3. Transfer Splash Pattern onto pin-dot card stock and yellow card stock.

4. Cut out card and designs. Embellish noisemaker as desired.

5. Adhere pin-dot splash onto noise-maker. Center and place foam dot on back of yellow splash. Place yellow splash on top of pin-dot splash.

6. Crease card and pop-up tab on perforation lines.

7. Adhere round balloon onto pop-up tab as desired. Adhere one heart balloon onto top edge of round balloon.

8. Adhere assorted colored balloons onto back of card.

9. Using black pen, draw balloon strings.

10. Cut 2¾" x 1½" rectangle from white card stock.

11. Cut mat ⅛" larger than rectangle all around from red card stock.

12. Using ink pad and rubber stamp, stamp image onto white rectangle. Center and adhere white rectangle onto red mat.

13. Adhere mat onto bottom inside of card.

14. Cut cover ⅛" larger than card all around from black cover stock. Fold in half widthwise.

15. Cut 4¼" x 3¾" rectangle from white card stock.

16. Adhere noisemaker onto white rectangle.

17. Using black pen and ruler, create border around rectangle. Write desired message on rectangle.

18. Adhere rectangle onto front of cover. Center and adhere cover onto card.

What's Up?

Materials & Tools

Card stock: blue; green; orange; red

Cover stock: white; yellow

Black felt-tipped pen

Border stickers: 1/16"

Orange marker

Patterns: Carrot (pg. 107); Multiple Pop-Up #2 (pg. 108)

Press-on letters for What's Up?

Ruler

Instructions

Refer to General Instructions on pages 5–13.

1. Enlarge Multiple Pop-Up #2 Pattern 44%. Transfer pattern onto white cover stock.

2. Transfer Carrot Pattern onto orange card stock. Repeat seven times.

3. Transfer top only of Carrot Pattern onto green card stock. Repeat seven times.

4. Cut out card and designs.

5. Crease card and pop-up tabs on perforation lines.

6. Using orange marker, shade carrots as desired.

7. Adhere green tops onto carrots.

8. Adhere carrots onto pop-up tabs.

9. Cut 4⅛" x 1⅛" rectangle from green card stock.

10. Using black pen and ruler, create border around rectangle. Write desired message on rectangle.

11. Adhere rectangle onto bottom inside of card. Place border stickers around top and bottom edges of card.

12. Cut 7½" x 10½" cover from yellow cover stock. Fold in half widthwise.

13. Adhere card onto inside of cover, matching folds.

14. Cut 4⅜" x 2½" rectangle from blue card stock.

15. Cut mat 1/16" larger than rectangle all around from red card stock.

16. Place letters on rectangle for What's Up?

17. Center and adhere rectangle onto mat. Center and adhere mat onto front of cover. Adhere remaining carrot onto front of mat as desired.

Invitation

Materials & Tools

Adhesive foam dots

Black felt-tipped pen

Black ink pad

Card stock: black/white checkered; green; orange; white; yellow

Cover stock: black

Craft punch: moon

Patterns: Ghost #2 (pg. 106); Multiple Pop-Up #1 (pg. 108); Tiny Pumpkin (pg. 106)

Rubber stamp: invitation

Ruler

Stickers: pumpkin; gerber daisy

Instructions

Refer to General Instructions on pages 5–13.

1. Enlarge Multiple Pop-Up Pattern 39%. Transfer pattern onto black cover stock.

2. Transfer Ghost #2 Pattern onto white card stock.

3. Transfer Tiny Pumpkin Pattern onto orange card stock. Repeat three times. Repeat four times with green card stock.

4. Cut out card and designs. Embellish pumpkins.

5. Crease card and pop-up tabs on perforation lines.

6. Adhere pumpkins onto pop-up tabs as desired. Place pumpkin sticker on remaining pop-up tab.

7. Cut 6" x 9" cover from from checkered card stock.

8. Cut cover ⅛" larger than checkered cover all around from black cover stock. Center and adhere checkered cover onto black cover, creating two-sided cover. Fold in half widthwise. Center and adhere card to cover.

9. Cut 2⅞" x 1½" rectangle from white card stock. Cut mat 1⁄16 larger than rectangle all around from orange card stock.

10. Using black ink pad and rubber stamp, stamp image onto rectangle.

Fill in information as desired. Center and adhere onto mat.

11. Adhere mat onto bottom left inside of card.

12. Cut 3¾" x 1" rectangle from yellow card stock.

13. Cut mat ¼" larger than rectangle all around from orange card stock.

14. Using black pen and ruler, create border around rectangle and around mat. Write desired message on rectangle.

15. Center and adhere rectangle onto mat. Adhere mat onto left top corner of card cover.

16. Cut two 1⁄16" x 6" and two 1⁄16" x 4½" strips from orange card stock Adhere strips around all four sides on front of cover.

17. Using craft punch, punch out four moons. Adhere one moon onto each front corner of cover.

18. Adhere one ghost onto front of cover. Place foam dots behind remaining ghost. Place ghost onto front of cover, overlapping first ghost.

19. Place daisy sticker in ghost's hand.

For:_____
When:_____
Where:_____Time:____
RSVP:_____

Photo Cards

Adding a photograph to a card instantly personalizes the greeting. Even the simplest of cards becomes more special with the inclusion of a photograph.

These Photo Cards are created with paper or cover stock that is two-sided—the two colors or patterns being compatible, but not identical.

The photograph at right shows the front and back of the card made from two-sided card stock before creasing on perforation lines.

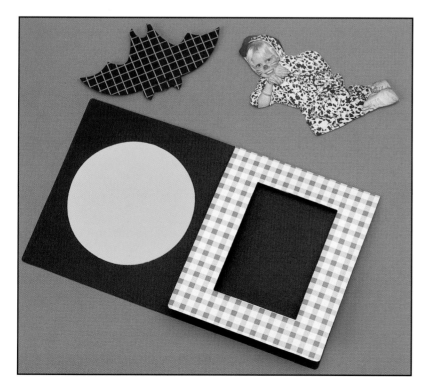

It is easy to create two-sided paper, using spray adhesive, adhesive sheets, or a Xyron machine that applies adhesive to full sheets of paper. Two-sided card stock is also available as well as two-sided gift wrap.

Once the paper is two-sided, the Picture Frame Fold Up is cut and creased on the perforation lines. The addition of themed designs or stickers and fancy pens is all that is needed for a super simple Photo Card. See photograph at left.

These Photo Cards fold flat for mailing, but sit up perfectly when removed from the envelope.

Springtime

Materials & Tools

Card stock: assorted coordinating patterns; cream/green patterned, two-sided

Double-sided tape

Pattern: Picture Frame Fold Up Card (pg. 110)

Photograph

Stickers: bow; floral

Instructions

Refer to General Instructions on pages 5–13.

1. Enlarge Picture Frame Fold Up Card Pattern 74%. Transfer pattern onto two-sided card stock.

2. Cut out card. Using craft knife, cut out frame opening.

3. Fold card on perforation lines.

4. Crop photograph to fit into frame as desired. Tape photograph to back of frame visible through frame. Tape sides and bottom of frame to back of card.

5. Cut 3" x 2" rectangle and 3" x 1" rectangle from assorted card stocks. Butt edges of rectangles together adhere onto inside front of cover. See photograph above.

6. Place floral sticker on top of mat. Place bow sticker on inside edges of rectangles.

SERINA

Halloween

Materials & Tools

Adhesive foam dots

Card stock: black patterned; black/orange/ white patterned, two-sided; yellow

Double-sided tape

Hole punch: ⅛"

Patterns: Bat (pg. 110); Picture Frame Fold Up Card (pg. 110)

Photograph

Press-on letters for desired message: ⅜"

Tiny star stickers (optional)

Instructions

Refer to General Instructions on pages 5–13.

1. Enlarge Picture Frame Fold Up Card Pattern 74%. Transfer pattern onto two-sided card stock.

2. Transfer Bat Pattern onto black patterned card stock.

3. Cut out card and designs. Using craft knife, cut out frame opening.

4. Crease card on perforation lines.

5. Cut 3"-diameter circle from yellow card stock.
Continued on page 42.

Continued from page 41.

6. Adhere a piece of yellow card stock onto inside of back cover behind frame opening.

7. Crop photograph to fit inside frame as desired. Tape photograph to inside back of card so it appears to sit on edge of frame. Tape sides and bottom of frame to inside back of card.

8. Adhere circle onto inside front of cover for moon.

9. Using hole punch, punch two circles from yellow card stock. Adhere circles onto bat for eyes.

10. Place foam dots on back of bat. Place bat on moon.

11. Center and place letters below moon for desired message. Tip: If desired message contains an "i"(s), dot with tiny star sticker(s).

Happy Hanukkah

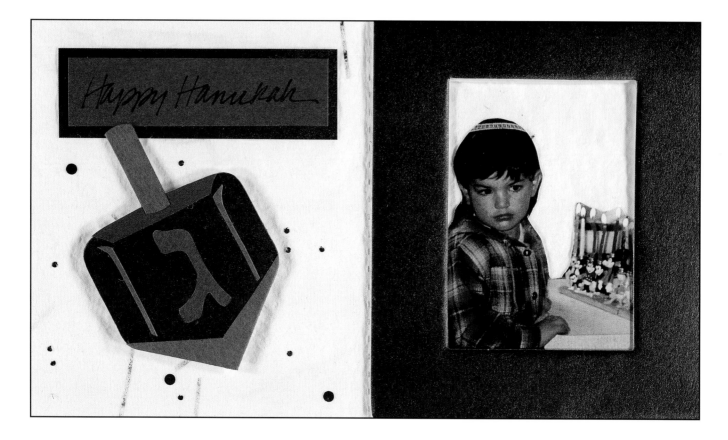

Materials & Tools

Adhesive foam dots

Card stock: dk. brown; lt. brown; gold metallic; gold metallic/white patterned, two-sided; purple

Double-sided tape

Gold metallic pen

Patterns: Dreidel (pg. 110); Picture Frame Fold Up Card (pg. 110)

Instructions

Refer to General Instructions on pages 5–13.

1. Enlarge Picture Frame Fold Up Card Pattern 74%. Transfer pattern onto two-sided card stock.

2. Transfer Dreidel Pattern onto metallic card stock.

3. Cut out card and designs. Using craft knife, cut out frame opening. Embellish dreidel as desired with dk. brown and lt. brown card stock.

4. Crease frame on perforation lines.

5. Adhere embellishments onto dreidel as desired.

6. Crop photograph to fit into frame as desired. Tape photograph to back of frame, visible through frame. Tape sides and bottom of frame to back of card.

7. Cut 2¾" x ¾" rectangle from purple card stock.

8. Using gold pen, write desired message on rectangle.

9. Cut mat ⅛" larger than rectangle all around from metallic card stock. Center and adhere rectangle onto mat. Center and adhere mat ¼" down from front top edge of card.

10. Place foam dots on back of dreidel. Place dreidel at left front of cover. Center and adhere message above dreidel.

These Photo Cards are created so that they will stand up when folded. What a quick and easy way to decorate a desk or bedside table.

Window Cards

The cover of a Window Card has an opening that allows some of the decorative elements inside of the card to show through. The size and shape of the window can vary.

A craft knife is the most effect way to cut out the window. Note: A ruler helps in keeping a straight edge. See photograph at right.

It is also effective to double or triple the number of folds so that multiple window openings can overlap each other on the front of the card. See Multiple Window Cards below.

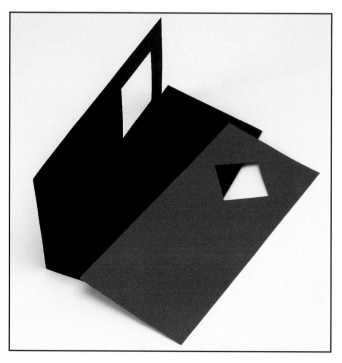

Multiple Window Cards

The Geometric Tri-Fold is folded into thirds so that one window opening remains on the front of cover, the second window opening shows through the first, and the base is solid. The folds of a Multiple Window Card can be lined with a different color. See photograph at left.

Too Cool

Materials & Tools

Adhesive foam dots

Card stock: black; craft; red

Craft knife

Pattern: Tiny Heart (pg. 109);

Pens: black felt-tipped; gold metallic

Ruler

Tiny gold star stickers (3)

Instructions

Refer to General Instructions on pages 5–13.

1. Transfer Tiny Heart Pattern onto red card stock. Repeat five times.

2. Cut out designs.

3. Cut 9⅛" x 6¼" rectangle from black card stock. Repeat with craft card stock.

4. Adhere black card stock onto craft card stock for two-sided card stock. Black is outside. Fold in half widthwise.

5. Using craft knife cut 2¾" square in card. See photograph.

6. Using black pen and ruler, create border through window on inside of card, slightly smaller than window.

7. Using gold pen, write desired messages on hearts.

8. Place foam dots on back of some of hearts. Place hearts inside border, overlapping hearts as desired.

9. Place gold star stickers on front of cover. See photograph.

Birthday Card

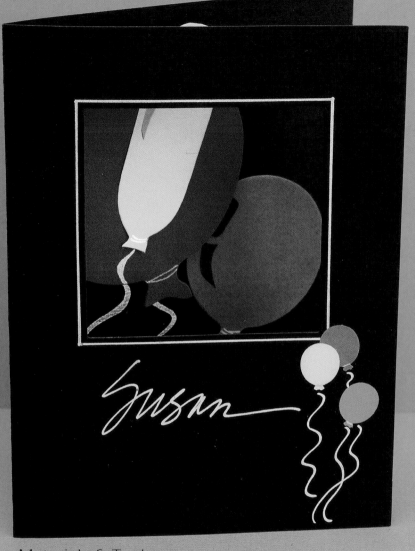

Materials & Tools

Adhesive foam dots

Card stock: assorted colors

Cover stock: black

Craft knife

Craft punch: balloon, small

Pattern: Balloons (pg. 113)

Ruler

Silver metallic pen

Instructions

Refer to General Instructions on pages 5–13.

1. Transfer Balloons Pattern as desired onto assorted colored card stock.

2. Cut out designs.

3. Cut 9⅛" x 6¼" rectangle from black cover stock. Fold in half widthwise.

4. Using craft knife, cut out 2¾" square in card. See photograph.

5. Draw highlights for balloons onto assorted colored card stock. Cut out highlights. Adhere highlights onto balloons.

6. Adhere oval balloon onto large balloon.

7. Place foam dots on back of large balloon. Place balloon on inside of card, visible through window.

8. Adhere remaining balloon onto inside of card.

9. Using silver pen, draw balloon strings. Close card.

10. Using silver pen and ruler, create border around window. Write desired message on front of card.

11. Using craft punch, punch balloons from assorted colored card stock. Adhere balloons onto front of card.

12. Using silver pen, draw balloon strings.

Swim Party

Materials & Tools

Card stock: assorted colors; white; yellow

Cover stock: blue

Craft knife

Patterns: Fin (pg.112); Snorkel and Mask (pg. 112)

Pens: blue felt-tipped; silver metallic

Plastic page protector

Instructions

Refer to General Instructions on pages 5–13.

1. Transfer Fin Pattern onto assorted colored card stock.

2. Transfer Snorkel and Mask Pattern onto assorted colored card stock. Repeat two times.

3. Cut out designs.

4. Cut 9⅛" x 6¼" rectangle from blue cover stock. Fold in half widthwise.

5. Using craft knife, cut out 2¾" square in card. See photograph.

6. Sandwich strip of plastic cut from plastic page protector between card stock masks. Match and adhere together. Adhere completed mask onto snorkel.

7. Cut 4¼" x 6" rectangle from yellow card stock. Adhere rectangle onto inside of card.

8. Cut 3½" x 2" rectangle from white card stock. Using blue pen, write party information on rectangle. Adhere rectangle onto inside bottom of card.

9. Adhere fin onto inside of card, visible through window.

10. Using silver pen, write desired message on front of card.

11. Adhere snorkel and mask onto front of card, overlapping window.

Merry Christmoose

Materials & Tools

Card stock: red; white

Craft knife

Felt-tipped pens: assorted colors

Patterns: Accordion Fold #1 (pg. 103); Moose (pg. 112)

Transparent tape

Instructions

Refer to General Instructions on pages 5–13.

1. Enlarge Accordion Fold #1 Pattern 34%. Transfer pattern onto red card stock.

2. Transfer Moose Pattern onto white card stock. Repeat two times.

3. Cut out Accordion Fold and designs.

4. Cut two 5½" x 8" covers from red card stock for front and back.

5. Using craft knife, cut 4" square in one cover.

6. Crease folds on perforation lines, creating pleats. Cut accordion fold into two sections to make sides of card. Note: Each section should have three pleats with a tab on each end.

7. Tape one end of fold on inside edge of front cover. Repeat for remaining fold at opposite edge of front cover. See photograph at right.

8. Adhere one moose onto inside front cover, visible through window.

9. Adhere second moose onto 5¼" x 3" rectangle. Tape rectangle into first pleat, facing moose in opposite direction of first moose. See photograph at left.

10. Adhere third moose onto 5¼" x 3" rectangle. Tape rectangle into second pleat, facing second moose in opposite direction.

11. Tape one end of fold on inside edge of back cover. Repeat for remaining fold at opposite edge of back cover. See photograph at left.

12. Cut 4" x 2" rectangle from white card stock.

13. Using assorted felt-tipped pens, write desired message on rectangle. Decorate as desired. Adhere rectangle below window onto front of card.

Rose
Window

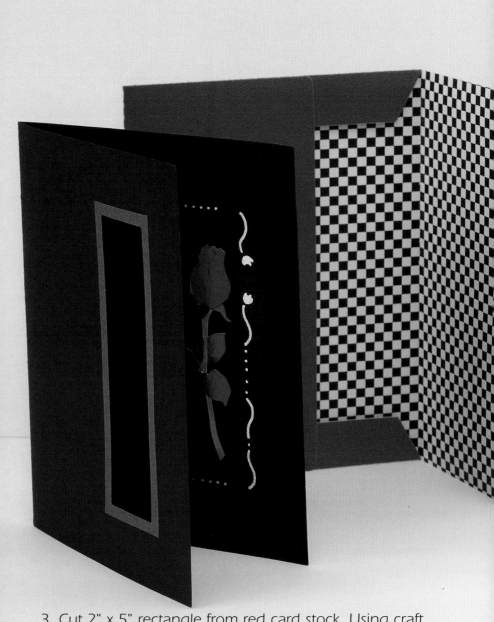

Materials & Tools

Card stock: red

Cover stock: black

Craft knife

Rose sticker

Ruler

Silver metallic pen

Instructions

Refer to General Instructions on pages 5–13.

1. Cut 6¼" x 9¼" rectangle from black cover stock. Fold in half widthwise.

2. Using craft knife, cut out 1½" x 4½" window. See photograph.

3. Cut 2" x 5" rectangle from red card stock. Using craft knife, cut out inside of rectangle, leaving red frame.

4. Adhere red frame onto window. See photograph.

5. Center and adhere rose sticker visible through window.

6. Using silver pen and ruler, create border around rose.

Feeling Down?

Materials & Tools

Black felt-tipped pen

Card stock: black; green; magenta; orange; yellow

Cover stock: blue

Craft knife

Craft punches: stem border; sun

Hole punch: ¼"

Pattern: Window Card #8 (pg. 111)

Ruler

Instructions

Refer to General Instructions on pages 5–13.

1. Cut 6¼" x 9¼" rectangle from blue cover stock. Fold in half widthwise.

2. Transfer Window Card #8 Pattern onto blue cover stock. See photograph.

3. Using craft knife, cut out window.

4. Use window shape to create a narrow border from magenta card stock. Cut out shape.

5. Adhere border onto window.

6. Using craft punch, punch out seven suns from yellow card stock. Repeat seven times on orange card stock.

7. Using hole punch, punch seven circles from black card stock.

8. Overlap and adhere one yellow sun onto one orange sun, creating sunflowers. Note: Sunflowers can be cut in half for a different look.

9. Center and adhere black circles onto sunflowers.

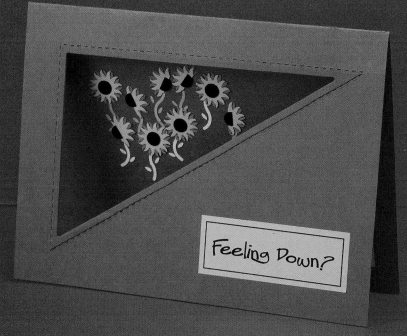

10. Using craft punch, punch out seven stems from green card stock.

11. Cut 2½" x 6¼" rectangle from yellow card stock.

12. Using black pen and ruler, create border around rectangle. Write desired message on rectangle.

13. Adhere rectangle ½" up from bottom front edge of card.

Baby Announcement

Materials & Tools

Burgundy ink pad

Card stock: assorted patterns; burgundy

Cover stock: cream

Craft knife

Craft punch: feet

Gold metallic pen

Patterns: Baby Rattle (pg. 112); Geometric
 Tri-Fold #2 (pg. 111)

Rubber stamp: baby announcement

Ruler

Instructions

Refer to General Instructions on pages 5–13.

1. Enlarge Geometric Tri-Fold #2 Pattern 56%. Transfer pattern onto cream cover stock.

2. Transfer Baby Rattle Pattern onto patterned card stock.

3. Cut out card and design. Using craft knife, cut out windows.

4. Crease card on perforation lines, folding in second layer of card first.

5. Using gold pen and ruler, create border around square window on front of card.

6. Line second layer of card with the diamond opening with complementary patterned card stock.

7. Line each section of inside of card with burgundy card stock, leaving cream border around each section.

8. Cut 3¼" x 4¾" rectangle from cream cover stock.

9. Using gold pen and ruler, create border around rectangle.

10. Using rubber stamp and burgundy ink pad, stamp image on rectangle. Fill in information as desired.

11. Using burgundy ink pad and your thumb, stamp image of your thumb on cream cover stock. Repeat. Using craft punch, punch out two feet from stamped thumb prints.

12. Center and adhere feet onto inside center section of card, visible through window.

13. Using gold pen, trace around feet as desired.

14. Adhere baby rattle onto front of card below square window.

Our New Baby

Name..
Date...
Time...
Weight...
Length...
Parents..

Dad

Materials & Tools

Black felt-tipped pen

Card stock: black; black/white pin-dot; blue; green; red; white; yellow

Cover stock: craft

Craft knife

Patterns: Fishing Pole (pg. 113); Geometric Tri-Fold #2 (pg. 111); Lollipop Alphabet for DAD (pg. 125); Tiny Fish (pg. 113)

Ruler

Instructions

Refer to General Instructions on pages 5–13.

1. Enlarge Geometric Tri-Fold #2 Pattern 56%. Transfer pattern onto craft card stock.

2. Transfer Fishing Pole onto black card stock.

3. Transfer Lollipop Alphabet Pattern for DAD onto pin-dot card stock. Note: Enlarge letters as desired.

4. Transfer Tiny Fish Pattern onto green card stock. Repeat with yellow card stock.

5. Cut out card and designs. Embellish fishing pole as desired. Using craft knife, cut out windows.

6. Crease card on perforation lines, folding in second layer of card first.

7. Using black pen and ruler, create border around square window on front of card.

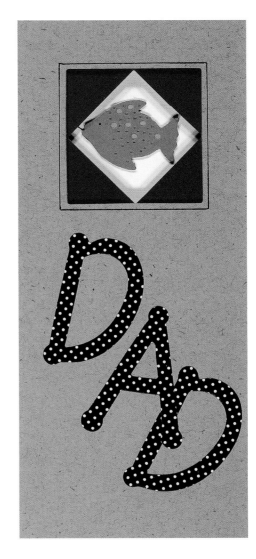

8. Line second layer of card with diamond opening with red card stock.

9. Line inside center of card with white card stock.

10. Using craft knife, poke holes in green fish, varying sizes. Using black pen, draw one eye on green fish.

11. Adhere green fish onto top of yellow fish. Center and adhere fish onto inside center of card, visible through window.

12. Adhere fishing pole onto inside center of card. Using black pen, draw fishing line from pole to fish's mouth as desired.

13. Cut 2" x ¾" rectangle from red card stock.

14. Using black pen and ruler, create border around rectangle. Write desired message on rectangle.

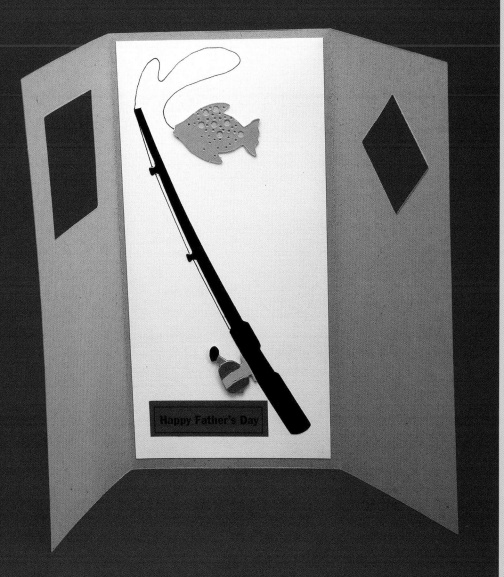

15. Adhere rectangle onto bottom inside center of card.

16. Adhere "Dad" below square window onto front of card.

Thank You

Materials & Tools

Black felt-tipped pen

Card stock: assorted patterns; craft; cream; leaf patterned (solid on reverse side)

Craft knife

Patterns: Geometric Tri-Fold #2 (pg.111); Tiny Heart (pg.109)

Ruler

Instructions

Refer to General Instructions on pages 5–13.

1. Enlarge Geometric Tri-Fold #2 Pattern 56%. Transfer pattern onto leaf patterned card stock.

2. Transfer Tiny Heart Pattern onto red patterned card stock.
Continued on page 56.

Continued from page 55.

3. Cut out card and design. Using craft knife, cut out windows from card.

4. Crease card on perforation lines, folding in second layer of card first.

5. Line second layer of card with diamond opening with craft card stock.

6. Cut 1¾" x ¾" rectangle from leaf patterned card stock.

7. Cut mat ⅟₁₆" larger than rectangle from cream card stock.

8. Cut second mat ⅟₁₆" larger than first mat from craft card stock.

9. Center and adhere smaller mat onto larger mat.

10. Using black pen, write desired message onto rectangle. Center and adhere rectangle onto mat.

11. Using black pen and ruler, create border around rectangle on mat.

12. Center and adhere heart onto inside center fold of card, visible through window.

13. Using black pen and ruler, create diamond-shaped border around heart.

Vellum Cards

Vellum is a specialty paper product that helps to create a particularly unique effect in card making. It is available in a variety of weights, colors, and textures with some being more "see-through" than others. See photograph at right.

It is easy to run vellum through a computer printer or color copy machine, making it possible to copy a photograph or print an entire wedding event onto vellum. See photographs below.

In each case, the vellum's filmy quality allows the item that is placed beneath to show through in a very special way.

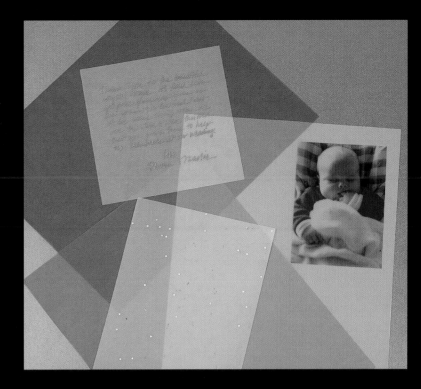

MARLIE

Running vellum through a color copier or computer printer will result in considerable savings as compared to a commercial printer. It is possible to print the text on vellum which sits over the photograph or color copy the photograph onto vellum which sits over the text.

Materials & Tools

Black felt-tipped pen

Card stock: beige patterned; lt. brown; dk. camel; lt. camel; white

Craft knife

Floral sticker

Pattern: Window Card #5 (pg. 114)

Ruler

Talcum powder

Vellum

Instructions

Refer to General Instructions on pages 5–13.

1. Enlarge Window Card #5 Pattern 65%. Transfer pattern onto beige patterned card stock. Cut out card. Using craft knife, cut out windows.

2. Transfer area between perforated lines for windowpanes onto white card stock. Cut out design. Using craft knife, cut out windows.

3. Crease card on perforation lines.

4. Sandwich vellum between white windowpanes and windowpanes on card. Match and adhere.

We've Moved

5. Cut 3¼" x 1" rectangle from lt. brown card stock.

6. Using black pen and ruler, create border around rectangle.

7. Adhere rectangle under window. Open center window. Place floral sticker on top edge of rectangle, extending over window.

8. Using fingers, brush powder on back side of sticker where it extends over window box.

9. Cut 4⅜" x 6" rectangle from lt. camel card stock. Center and adhere rectangle onto inside back of card.

10. Cut 3" x ½" rectangle from lt. camel card stock.

11. Using black pen, write desired message on rectangle.

12. Cut mat 1/16" larger than rectangle all around from dk. camel card stock.

13. Center and adhere rectangle onto mat. Center and adhere mat onto top inside of back card.

Love

Materials & Tools

Black embroidery floss

Card stock: black;
  cream; gold metallic

Cover stock: black

Craft knife

Hole punch: ¹⁄₁₆"

Gold metallic pen

Pattern: Tiny Heart (pg. 109)

Ruler

Vellum or handmade transparent paper

Instructions

Refer to General Instructions on pages 5–13.

1. Cut 3" x 1½" rectangle from metallic card stock. Transfer Tiny Heart Pattern onto metallic rectangle. Repeat. Using craft knife, carefully cut out design, saving rectangle.

2. Cut 6⅜" x 9⅜" cover from black cover stock. Fold in half widthwise.

3. Center and adhere rectangle onto cover. Using gold pen and ruler, create border around rectangle.

4. Cut 6" x 9" cover from vellum or handmade paper. Fold cover in half widthwise. Place vellum cover over black cover, matching folds.

5. Using hole punch, pierce one hole 1¾" in from end of fold. Repeat for remaining end of fold through both vellum and card.

6. Cut 6" x 4½" rectangle from cream card stock for inside of card.

7. Center and adhere rectangle onto inside back of cover.

8. Cut 20" piece of embroidery floss. Thread each end of floss through holes to inside of card. Tie into bow.

Materials & Tools

Card stock: dk. camel; lt. camel; cream

Color copy of photograph: 5" x 4" (Option #2)

Color copy of photograph on vellum: 5" x 4" (Option #1)

Craft knife

Double-sided tape

Floral stickers (2)

Patterns: Overlapping Card A (pg. 115); Overlapping Card B (pg. 115)

Engagement Announcement

Instructions

Refer to General Instructions on pages 5–13.

1. Enlarge Overlapping Card A Pattern 51%. Enlarge Overlapping Card B Pattern 51%.

2. Transfer Card A Pattern onto dk. camel card stock.

3. Transfer Card B Pattern onto lt. camel card stock.

4. Cut out cards. Using craft knife, cut slits. Fold cards in half widthwise.

5. Overlap and tape one half of each card to each other. See photograph.

Option #1

6. Print desired message to fit on 5¼" x 4¼" rectangle from cream card stock. Cut 5¼" x 4¼" rectangle with desired message.

7. Center and adhere top edge of vellum color copy of photograph onto top edge of rectangle. Center and adhere rectangle onto center inside of card.

8. Place bottom of floral sticker on top edge of rectangle.

9. Close card with pointed end sliding through bottom slits. Place floral sticker at end of flap to secure.

Option #2

10. Cut 5¼" x 4¼" rectangle from cream card stock.

11. Center and adhere color copy of photograph onto rectangle. Center and adhere onto inside of card.

12. Print desired message to fit 5½" x 4½" rectangle of vellum. Cut 5½" x 4½" rectangle with message.

13. Place vellum over top of color copy. Place bottom of floral sticker at top center edge of vellum, attaching vellum to card.

14. Close card with pointed end sliding through bottom slits. Place floral sticker at end of flap to secure.

Darren Frederick Gogolan
and
Marlie Bennett Stewart
announce their
Engagement

The Wedding is planned for
early June
with a Honeymoon in Hawaii
They plan to reside in
Huntington Beach, California

Two options are shown for the same card: one with the photograph color-copied onto vellum and text printed on cream-colored paper, and the other with the text printed on vellum and the photograph color-copied onto cream-colored card stock.

Tie It Up Cards

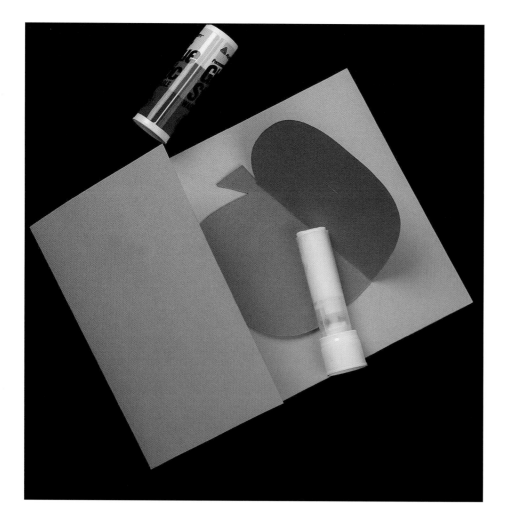

Tie It Up Cards are closed with a ribbon, string, or tie of some sort. Each card is folded on both sides and the card ends meet in the middle. A shape (geometric or decorative) is cut in pairs, folded identically and adhered over each end of the card. See photograph at left. This creates the look of one whole shape on the card front. It is possible to vary the look slightly by substituting a paper element that overlaps the middle seam in place of the ribbon.

This Tie It Up Card is decorated with red hearts and a single red rose sticker. It is the perfect card to tell the one that you love thanks for all they do.

Heart in a Diamond

Materials & Tools

Card stock: cream;
  dk. green; green
  flecked; green floral
  with cream back

Green felt-tipped pen

Ruler

Stickers: bow; floral;
  gold heart

Instructions

Refer to General Instructions on pages 5–13.

1. Cut 7¾" x 10 ¾" card from green floral card stock. Fold widthwise, meeting two ends in middle.

2. Cut two 3¾" squares from dk. green card stock.

3. Cut two squares ¹⁄₁₆" smaller than dk. green squares from green flecked card stock.

4. Center and adhere smaller squares onto larger squares. Fold squares in half diagonally.

5. Adhere inside half of each square to inside flaps, leaving outside half of squares loose. Close card.

6. Cut 3¼" x ¾" rectangle from green floral card stock.

7. Cut mat ¹⁄₁₆" larger than rectangle all around from cream card stock.

8. Cut 3" x ¹⁄₁₆" strip from dk. green card stock.

9. Center and adhere strip onto rectangle. Center and place heart sticker on strip.

Continued on page 64.

Continued from page 63.

10. Center and adhere rectangle onto mat. Center and adhere left half of mat onto left square, leaving rectangle loose on remaining side. See photograph on page 63.

11. Cut 3¾" x 4¼" rectangle from green flecked card stock.

12. Center and adhere rectangle ¾" down from top inside of card.

13. Using green pen and ruler, create border around rectangle. Place floral sticker over top edge of rectangle.

14. Cut 3¾" x ⅛" and 3¼" x ⅛" strips from dk. green card stock.

15. Center and adhere strips below rectangle as desired. Place bow sticker below strips.

Broken Heart

Materials & Tools

Card stock: blue; cream; cream/blue patterned; yellow; yellow/white checkered

Pattern: Bandage (pg. 115)

Stickers: floral; tiny heart

Instructions

Refer to General Instructions on pages 5–13.

1. Transfer Bandage Pattern onto yellow card stock.

2. Cut out designs.

3. Cut 4¾" x 4¼" heart from yellow/white checkered card stock. Repeat.

4. Cut 9½" x 6" card from cream/blue patterned card stock that is plain on reverse side. Fold widthwise, meeting two ends in middle.

5. Fold hearts in half. Adhere inside half of each heart to inside flaps, leaving outside half loose. Close card.

6. Place floral sticker along bottom edge of heart on outside flap.

7. Cut mat from blue card stock ⅛" larger than bandage all around.

8. Adhere bandage onto mat. Place heart sticker on bandage. Adhere half of bandage onto heart, leaving other half loose.

9. Cut 5½" x 4¼" rectangle from yellow card stock.

10. Adhere rectangle onto inside middle of card. Place floral sticker at center top of rectangle.

Hi

Materials & Tools

Black felt-tipped pen

Brads (2)

Card stock: black; craft; red

Craft paper: black/craft patterned; black/gold metallic patterned; gold metallic

Double-sided tape

Embroidery thread (12")

Hole punch: ¼"

Press-on letters for Hi: 2"

Instructions

Refer to General Instructions on pages 5–13.

1. Draw 4" circle onto black/craft patterned craft paper. Repeat.

2. Draw 1" circle onto red card stock. Repeat.

3. Cut out designs.

4. Cut 11" x 8" card from craft card stock. Fold widthwise, meeting two ends in middle.

5. Cut two mats ¼" larger than large circles all around from black card stock. Adhere circles onto mats.

6. Cut two 2" squares from metallic gold craft paper. Adhere square onto each large circle.
Continued on page 66.

Continued from page 65.

7. Fold large circles in half so gold square on top is folded diagonally. Position large folded circles over card flaps. Close card.

8. Place small red circles on top of gold triangles. See photograph.

9. Using hole punch, punch hole through small circles, outside half of large circles, and flaps. Do not punch hole through inside half of circles.

13. Cut 2½" square from black/gold patterned craft paper.

14. Cut mat from metallic craft paper ⅛" larger than square all around. Adhere square onto mat.

15. Cut 7¾" x 5¼" rectangle from black card stock. Adhere rectangle to inside middle of card. Adhere matted square onto center top of rectangle.

16. Place letters inside square for Hi.

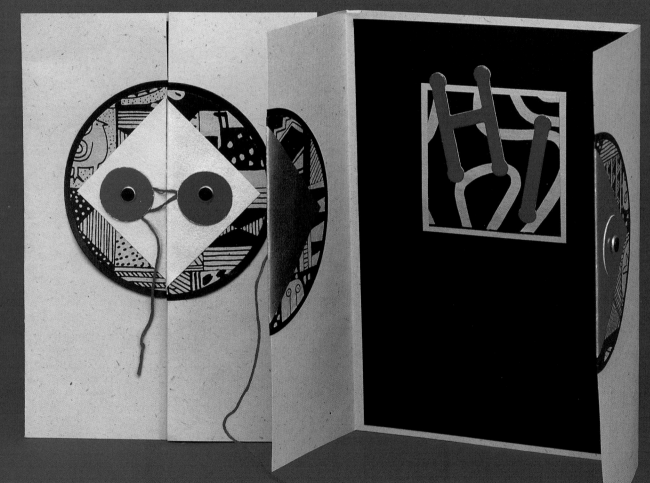

10. Insert brad through each hole. Bend ends to close.

11. Tape inside circles to flaps, covering brad ends.

12. Using black pen, color tops of brads.

17. Tie slip knot at one end of thread. Pull thread to close knot, under small red circle. Knot other end of thread. Wrap end around opposite brad to close card.

Halloween Invitation

Materials & Tools

Black felt-tipped pen

Black satin ribbon: ¼"-wide (1 yd.)

Card stock: black; green; orange; orange/white checkered; yellow

Craft knife

Orange craft paper

Patterns: Pumpkin (pg. 113); Tiny Pumpkin (pg. 106)

Instructions

Refer to General Instructions on pages 5–13.

1. Transfer Pumpkin Pattern onto orange craft paper. Repeat.

2. Transfer Tiny Pumpkin Pattern onto orange card stock. Repeat two times.

3. Transfer pumpkin's and tiny pumpkin's stems onto green card stock. Repeat.

4. Cut out designs.

5. Cut 14" x 5½" card from yellow card stock. Fold widthwise, meeting two ends in middle.

6. Adhere green pumpkin stems onto orange pumpkin stems.
Continued on page 68.

Continued from page 67.

7. Using craft knife, cut ¾" slit in right side of one pumpkin and left side of other pumpkin. See photograph on page 67.

8. Fold pumpkins in half widthwise. Adhere inside of each pumpkin to inside flaps of card, leaving outside half of pumpkins loose. Close card.

9. Cut 5¼" x 6¾" rectangle from checkered card stock. Adhere rectangle onto inside middle section of card.

10. Cut 2½" x 3½" rectangle from white card stock.

11. Using black pen, write party information on rectangle.

12. Cut 6¼" x 4½" rectangle from black card stock. Adhere to checkered paper. See photograph on page 67.

13. Adhere white rectangle onto bottom right corner of black rectangle. Adhere small pumpkins to black rectangle as desired.

14. Thread ribbon through left slit, around back, and through right slit. Tie ribbon in bow on front of card.

Christmas Star

Materials & Tools

Card stock: cream; gold metallic; green

Christmas floral sticker

Craft knife

Pattern: Primitive Star (pg. 113)

Pens: gold metallic; red felt-tipped

Red satin ribbon: ¼"-wide (24")

Ruler

Instructions

Refer to General Instructions on pages 5–13.

1. Transfer Primitive Star Pattern onto metallic card stock. Repeat.

2. Cut out designs.

3. Cut 8½" x 5½" card from green card stock. Fold widthwise, meeting two ends in middle.

4. Using craft knife, cut ¾" slit in right side of one star and left side of remaining star.

5. Fold stars in half lengthwise. Adhere inside portion of each star to each inside flap, leaving outside flaps of star loose. Close card.

6. Cut 1½" x ¼" and 3¾" x ¼" strips from metallic paper. Cut strips in half widthwise.

7. Adhere two shorter strips ¼" down from top edge of card, meeting in middle. Repeat for remaining strips and bottom edge of card. See photograph.

8. Using gold pen, dot around stars on outside flaps.

9. Cut 3½" x 4½" rectangle from cream card stock. Place floral sticker on center top of rectangle.

10. Using red pen and ruler, create border around rectangle below sticker.

11. Cut mat ⅛" larger than rectangle all around from metallic card stock.

12. Center and adhere rectangle onto mat. Adhere mat onto inside section of card.

13. Thread ribbon through left slit, around back, and through right slit. Tie ribbon in bow on front of card.

Envelope Cards

Sometimes it is handy to have the card and envelope combined into one neat, little package. This combination is called an envelope card.

The photograph at right shows how the envelope card is creased on perforation lines. The envelope is sealed with a sticker, cutout design, or die-cut, then unfolded to reveal the card, which is created directly onto the inside of the envelope.

It is also possible to cut the envelope from clear mylar (e.g. a page protector) so that the card sits separately inside and shows through the envelope. See page 74.

Note: When mailing square Envelope Cards, be certain to include extra postage stamps as needed.

This Envelope Card makes a great thank you card for bridal showers or weddings. Express your thoughts on a clear page protector, that is cut to fit over the color copy of the photograph. The top layer is held in place at the top with a floral sticker, which allows the recipient to lift the message for clearer view of the color-copied photograph beneath.

It's a Boy

On the card image: ITS A BOY

Justin Ames
7 LBS. 6 OZS. 21"
March 25, 1997

Materials & Tools

Black felt-tipped pen

Card stock: cream; blue flecked with cream back; blue patterned; yellow; yellow patterned

Patterns: Baby Booties (pg. 117); Envelope #3 (pg. 116); Smaller Puffy Star (pg. 114); Smaller Puffy Star Mat (pg. 114)

Press-on letters for desired message: ¼"

Instructions

Refer to General Instructions on pages 5–13.

1. Enlarge Envelope #3 Pattern 46%. Transfer onto blue flecked card stock with solid back.

2. Transfer Baby Booties Pattern onto blue patterned card stock. Repeat with yellow card stock.

3. Transfer Smaller Puffy Star Mat Pattern onto yellow card stock.

4. Transfer Smaller Puffy Star Pattern onto blue patterned paper.
Continued on page 72.

Continued from page 71.

5. Cut out card and designs.

6. Cut 4" x 1⅜" rectangle from yellow card stock.

7. Cut mat ⅟₁₆" larger than rectangle all around from blue flecked card stock.

8. Center and adhere rectangle onto mat. Center and adhere mat onto front of envelope for mailing address.

9. Cut 5⅜" square from cream card stock.

10. Cut 5¼" square from yellow patterned card stock.

11. Center and adhere smaller square onto larger square.

12. Cut out yellow shoe laces from baby bootie. Adhere shoe laces over blue patterned baby booties.

13. Adhere baby booties onto square as desired. Center and adhere square onto inside of card.

14. Cut 1½" x ¾" rectangle from cream card stock.

15. Using black pen, write birth inforamation on rectangle.

16. Cut mat ⅟₁₆" larger than rectangle from yellow card stock.

17. Cut second mat ⅟₃₂" larger than rectangle from blue flecked card stock.

18. Center and adhere rectangle onto yellow mat. Center and adhere smaller mat onto larger mat.

19. Place letters on baby bootie tops as desired.

20. Center and adhere smaller puffy star onto smaller puffy star mat.

21. Crease card on perforation lines.

22. Center and adhere puffy star where four corners of card meet to seal envelope closed.

Party Invitation

Materials & Tools

Black ink pad

Card stock: black; black/white checkered; green; red; white; yellow

Patterns: Envelope #3 (pg.116); Glass with Straws (pg. 116); Watermelon 1 (pg. 115); Watermelon 2 (pg. 115)

Rubber stamp: invitation

Ruler

Silver metallic pen

Instructions

Refer to General Instructions on pages 5–13.

1. Enlarge Envelope #3 Pattern 46%. Transfer pattern onto black cover stock.

2. Transfer Glass with Straws Pattern onto white card stock. Transfer area between perforated lines onto yellow card stock. Transfer straw onto red card stock.

3. Transfer Watermelon 1 Pattern onto green card stock. Repeat.

4. Transfer Watermelon 2 Pattern onto red card stock. Repeat. Repeat with black card stock. Repeat.

5. Cut out card and designs. Adhere red straws on top of straw. Using perforation as guide, adhere yellow lemonade onto glass. See photograph.

6. Cut 4" x 1⅝" rectangle from red card stock.

7. Center and adhere rectangle onto front of envelope for mailing address.

8. Using silver pen and ruler, create border around rectangle.

9. Cut 5⅞" x ½" rectangle from checkered card stock.

10. Cut mat ⅛" larger than rectangle from yellow card stock.

11. Cut second mat 1/16" larger than first mat all around from red card stock.

12. Center and adhere rectangle onto yellow mat. Center and adhere mat onto red mat.

13. Center and adhere mat ⅛" down onto top inside edge of card.

14. Using black ink pad and rubber stamp, stamp image onto glass. Note: If computer-generating invitation, print onto white card stock then transfer glass pattern around invitation.

15. Adhere glass onto left edge of card, extending straws into checkered border at top.

16. Trim black watermelon section 1/16" smaller than red watermelon section. Adhere sections together. Repeat for remaining watermelon sections.

17. Adhere red watermelon sections onto green watermelon sections, matching straight edges.

18. Adhere one watermelon onto bottom of card, overlapping glass.

19. Crease card on perforation lines.

20. Center and adhere remaining watermelon where four corners of card meet to seal envelope closed.

Thanks

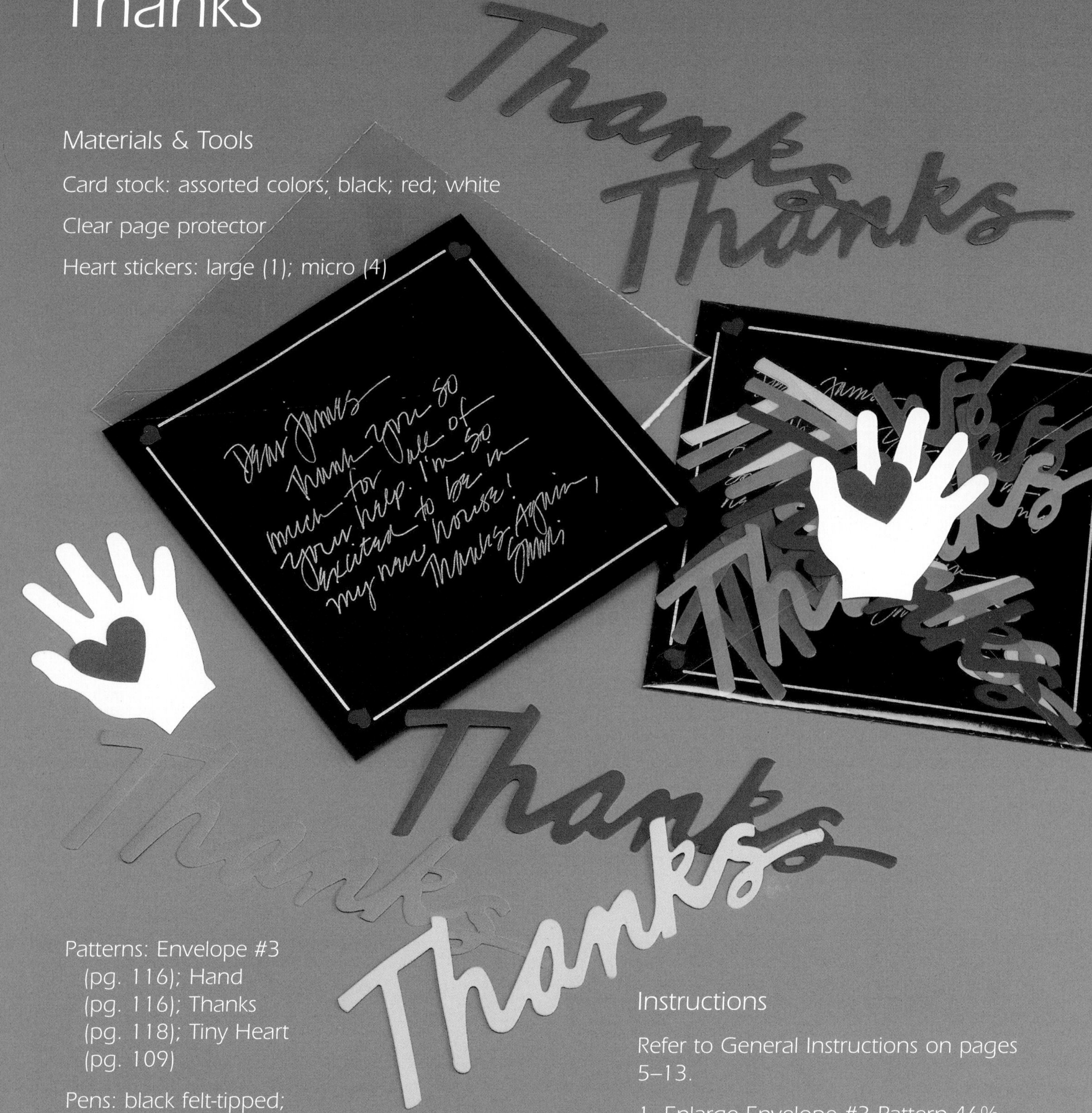

Materials & Tools

Card stock: assorted colors; black; red; white

Clear page protector

Heart stickers: large (1); micro (4)

Patterns: Envelope #3
    (pg. 116); Hand
    (pg. 116); Thanks
    (pg. 118); Tiny Heart
    (pg. 109)

Pens: black felt-tipped;
    silver metallic

Instructions

Refer to General Instructions on pages 5–13.

1. Enlarge Envelope #3 Pattern 46%. Transfer pattern onto clear page protector.

2. Transfer Thanks Pattern onto assorted colored card stock. Repeat six times.

3. Transfer Hand Pattern onto white card stock.

4. Transfer Tiny Heart Pattern onto red card stock.

5. Cut out envelope and designs.

6. Crease envelope on perforation lines.

7. Cut 5⅜" square card from black card stock.

8. Using silver pen and ruler, create border around card. Write desired message on card.

9. Place one micro heart sticker on each corner of card.

10. Using black pen, write recipient's address on large heart sticker. Center and place large heart sticker on back side of black card.

11. Using silver pen, dot around heart.

12. Place card into envelope with address information, facing opposite of flaps.

13. Place assorted thanks into envelope as desired.

14. Adhere heart between thumb and forefinger of hand.

15. Center and adhere hand where four corners of envelope meet to seal envelope closed.

I've Moved

Materials & Tools

Card stock: assorted colors; black; red; white

Clear page protector

Craft knife

Double-sided tape

Patterns: Curved Arrow (pg. 116); Envelope #2 (pg. 119); Lollipop Alphabet (pg.125); Tiny Check Mark (pg. 115)

Pen: black felt-tipped; silver metallic; white felt-tipped

Ruler

Tiny heart stickers (4)

Instructions

Refer to General Instructions on pages 5–13.

1. Enlarge Envelope #2 Pattern 58%.

2. Transfer Envelope #2 Pattern onto clear page protector.

3. Transfer Curved Arrow Pattern onto white card stock.

4. Transfer Lollipop Alphabet for MOVED onto assorted colored card stocks, making certain to transfer each letter onto a different color of card stock. Note: Enlarge letters for MOVED as desired.

5. Transfer Tiny Check Mark Pattern onto red card stock.

6. Cut out envelope and designs. Using craft knife, cut slit in envelope.

Continued on page 76.

Continued from page 75.

7. Crease envelope on perforations lines.

8. Tape and seal side flaps.

9. Cut 3⅜" x 6¼" card from black cover stock.

10. Using silver pen and ruler, create border around card. Place one tiny heart sticker on each corner of card.

11. Cut 2¾" x ¾" rectangle from black cover stock.

12. Using white pen and ruler, create border around rectangle.

13. Write "IT OUT" on rectangle, leaving space for the check mark. Note: This can also be computer-generated with reverse type. Because the background is black, the paper will disappear when it is adhered to the card.

14. Adhere check mark onto left edge of rectangle, creating message ✓ IT OUT. Center and adhere rectangle onto card. See photograph.

15. Using silver pen, write desired message below rectangle on card. Write recipient's name and address horizontally on back of card.

16. Place card in envelope with address information, facing opposite of flap.

17. Drop letters into envelope as desired.

18. Insert envelope flap inside slit. Center and adhere arrow onto top of slit to seal envelope closed.

Faux Embossed Cards

To emboss is to raise in relief, the surface of the card. Embossing adds a special touch of elegance to cards for all occasions.

Faux embossing is a shortcut that adds the beauty of embossing without the extra time.

Cut the embossed image from the same paper as the card on which it will sit. When the cut-out is fastened to the card, it gives the illusion of embossing because it is raised off the card surface. See photograph at left.

Beautiful pre-embossed card stock is also available in several different patterns. Create patterns from this paper, or use the paper as the card itself for an especially quick and easy elegance.

Embossing is particularly effective for wedding events, birth announcements, valentine and anniversary cards, or any time an elegant look is desired.

This Faux Embossed Card was created with pre-embossed card stock. Decorated with colored card stock and stickers, making greeting cards does not get any easier than this.

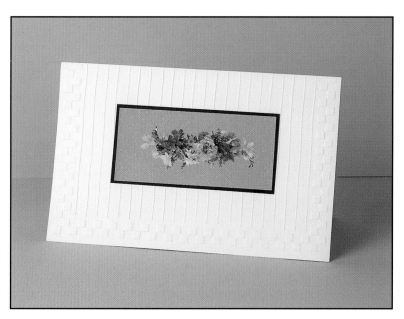

Gotta Have Heart

Materials & Tools

Card stock: cream;
   cream embossed;
   gold metallic; red

Cover stock: black

Gold metallic pen

Micro heart stickers (4)

Patterns: Heart #3A
   (pg. 118); Love
   (pg. 118)

Instructions

Refer to General Instructions on pages 5–13.

1. Transfer Heart #3A Pattern onto red card stock.

2. Transfer Love Pattern onto metallic card stock.

3. Cut out designs.

4. Cut 7" x 10" card from black cover stock. Fold in half widthwise.

5. Cut 4¼" x 6" rectangle from cream card stock.

6. Cut mat ¹⁄₁₆" larger than rectangle all around from metallic card stock.

7. Place micro heart stickers on top and bottom of rectangle. See photograph on facing page.

8. Center and adhere rectangle onto mat. Center and adhere mat onto inside of card.

9. Cut 3⅜" square from cream embossed card stock.

10. Cut mat ⅟₁₆" larger than square all around from metallic card stock.

11. Center and adhere heart onto square. Center and adhere square onto mat.

12. Center and adhere mat ½" down from top front of card.

13. Center and adhere Love below mat on front of card.

14. Using gold pen, dot around Love.

Love You

Materials & Tools

Black felt-tipped pen

Cover stock: craft; cream

Floral stickers: large;
  small

Pattern: Love (pg. 118)

Ruler

Instructions

Refer to General Instructions on pages 5–13.

1. Transfer Love Pattern onto cream card stock. Cut out design.

2. Cut 7" x 10" card from craft cover stock. Fold in half widthwise.

3. Cut 6" x 4" rectangle from cream card stock.

4. Cut fifteen ⅜" squares from cream card stock.

5. Adhere squares onto bottom of rectangle in checkerboard fashion. See photograph on page 79.

6. Center and adhere rectangle onto inside of card.

7. Using black pen and ruler, create border around rectangle.

8. Place small floral sticker on top inside edge of card, overlapping rectangle.

9. Cut 4⅞" x 3⅞" rectangle from cream card stock.

10. Center and adhere Love onto rectangle. Center and adhere rectangle onto front of card.

11. Using black pen and ruler, create border around rectangle.

12. Place large floral sticker on top edge front of card, slightly overlapping rectangle.

The faux embossed technique allows for other elements like checkered heart shown below to sit between the embossed element and the card.

Silly Goose

Materials & Tools

Black felt-tipped pen

Bow stickers: large; medium

Card stock: blue flecked; cream

Colored pencils

Cover stock: blue patterned with solid back

Pattern: Goose (pg. 119)

Instructions

Refer to General Instructions on pages 5–13.

1. Transfer Goose Pattern onto cream card stock.

2. Cut out design.

3. Cut 8" x 10¾" card from cover stock.

4. Fold cover stock in half widthwise.

5. Cut 4" x ⅜" rectangle from blue flecked card stock.

6. Center and adhere rectangle 1" down from inside top of card.

Continued on page 82.

Continued from page 81.

7. Place medium bow on top edge of blue flecked rectangle, overlapping rectangle.

8. Cut 4¾" x 5¾" rectangle from cream card stock.

9. Using black pen and ruler, create border around rectangle. Create lines for desired message.

10. Center and adhere rectangle onto inside of card, below blue flecked rectangle.

11. Using colored pencils, lightly shade beak, feet and eye of goose. Place large bow sticker on goose's neck.

12. Cut 3⅜" x 4¼" rectangle from cream card stock.

13. Center and adhere goose onto cream rectangle.

14. Cut two 3¼" x ⅛" strips from blue flecked card stock. Cut two 4" x ⅛" strips from blue flecked card stock.

15. Adhere strips ⅛" in from edges of cream rectangle, overlapping corners creating border. See photograph on page 81.

16. Cut 2¼" x ⅛" strip from blue flecked card stock.

17. Center and adhere strip below goose inside of border.

18. Adhere rectangle to front of card 1" below top edge of card.

Season's Greetings

Materials & Tools

Card stock: cream; gold metallic

Cover stock: red

Craft punch: tiny star

Pattern: Tree Border (pg. 119)

Self-adhesive paper: gold metallic; red

Tiny heart stickers (4)

Instructions

Refer to General Instructions on pages 5–13.

1. Transfer Tree Border Pattern onto cream card stock.

2. Cut out design.

3. Cut 6½" x 9½" card from red cover stock. Fold in half widthwise.

4. Cut 3¾" x 5½" rectangle from cream card stock.

5. Cut mat ⅜" larger than rectangle all around from metallic card stock.

6. Cut two 3" x ¹⁄₁₆" and one 2½" x ¹⁄₁₆" strips from red card stock.

7. Center and adhere one 3" strip ¹⁄₁₆" from top edge of rectangle. Repeat with other 3" at bottom. Center and adhere remaining strip above bottom strip. Place star stickers on ends of top and bottom strips. See photograph.

8. Center and adhere rectangle onto mat. Center and adhere mat onto inside of card.

9. Cut 4½" x 6¼" rectangle from cream card stock.

10. Cut 3¾" x ¹⁄₁₆" and 4" x ¹⁄₁₆" strips from metallic card stock.

11. Center and adhere 4" strip ¼" up from bottom edge of rectangle. Center and adhere remaining strip ⅛" above bottom strip.

12. Center and adhere tree onto rectangle.

13. Using craft punch, punch out 12 stars from gold and red self-adhesive paper.

14. Place stars on tree and rectangle as desired.

Spiral Mobile Cards

A Spiral Mobile Card is one that arrives in a flat envelope and magically suspends from the ceiling for a unique and special three-dimensional greeting.

A spiral is used as the mechanism that holds each of the dangling elements. This type of mobile virtually eliminates the difficulties associated with balancing all of the elements and keeping the threads untangled. Plus, the mobile lies flat, making it easy to slide into an envelope and send through the mail.

To slide it into an envelope, simply lay the mobile flat on a sheet of paper, slide the paper into the envelope and remove the paper, leaving the spiral mobile inside.

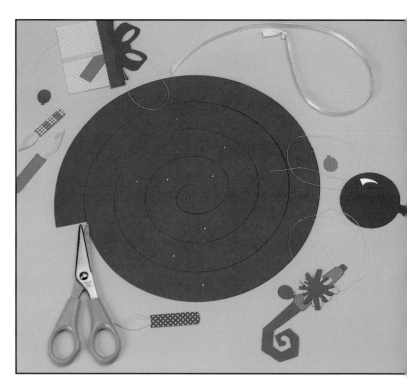

Envelopes are available in a variety of colors and 9" x 12" is the perfect size for holding larger Spiral Mobile Cards. An A-6 envelope is just the right size for the smaller spiral mobiles.

It is helpful to leave the thread long while fastening the shapes to the spiral. See photograph at left. When stickers are used to hold the thread, barely press down on each sticker while arranging the shapes. This allows the thread to be raised or lowered easily. When the arrangement is complete, press the stickers down firmly to hold the shapes in place and trim any excess thread.

Valentine Sweetheart

Materials & Tools

Card stock: assorted red/white patterned; gray; red; tan; white

Craft knife

Hole punch: ¼"

Patterns: Cherub (pg. 121); Heart #1A (pg. 120); Primitive Hearts (pg. 107); Small Heart (pg. 119); Spiral (pg. 120); Tiny Heart (pg. 109);

Pens: black felt-tipped; silver metallic

Photograph

Poster board: black

Push pin

Red micro heart stickers

Red ink pad

Red satin ribbon: ¼"-wide (1 yd.)

White thread

Instructions

Refer to General Instructions on pages 5–13.

1. Enlarge Spiral Pattern 55%. Transfer pattern onto black poster board.

2. Transfer Heart #1A Pattern onto red card stock. Cut two. Note: This pattern will generate a heart frame and a heart.

3. Transfer Small Heart Pattern and Tiny Heart Pattern onto patterned card stocks. Cut two of each.

4. Transfer Cherub Pattern onto tan card stock. Cut two. Repeat with white card stock. Cut two.

5. Transfer Primitive Hearts Pattern onto assorted colored card stocks. Cut two.

6. Cut out spiral. Using craft knife, cut out inside heart from Heart #1A. Embellish cherub's wings with gray card stock on white wings.

7. Using black pen, draw eyes on cherubs.

8. Using ink pad, lightly ink finger tip and gently press finger on cherubs' cheeks.

9. Adhere black piece of card stock onto back of one heart frame. Using silver pen, write desired message on black section of heart frame.

10. Crop photograph to fit in heart frame. Adhere photograph behind heart frame with black heart as backing.

11. Using hole punch, punch hole in center of spiral. Cut 28" piece of ribbon. Insert ribbon through hole. Knot at one end to hold in place. Note: The ribbon will suspend the spiral from the ceiling.

12. Using push pin, pierce tiny holes in spiral to suspend designs.

13. Cut seven pieces of thread in desired lengths to hang designs from spiral.

14. Sandwich one end of thread vertically between each pair. Match and adhere pairs together.

15. Insert remaining end of thread through pierced holes. Repeat for all designs. Adhere thread onto spiral with micro heart stickers.

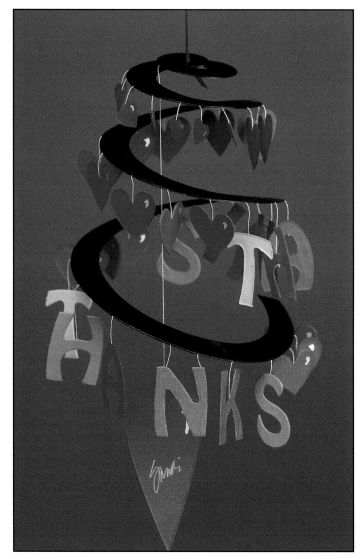

Above is another idea for a Spiral Mobile Card. Thread can be sandwiched between two matching designs which are then draped over the edges of the spiral. Each design is taped to top and an extra spiral is cut out to cover all of the tape.

Birthday Wishes

Materials & Tools

Black felt-tipped pen

Card stock: assorted colors; hot-pink; yellow

Craft punch: tiny balloon

Hole punch: ¼"

Patterns: Balloons (pg. 109); Candles (pg. 106); Gift Tag (pg. 120); Gift with Ribbon (pg. 120); Noisemaker (pg. 109); Numbers (pg.107); Spiral (pg. 120); Splash (pg. 109)

Poster board: blue

Push pins

White thread

Yellow satin ribbon: ⅛"-wide

Instructions

Refer to General Instructions on pages 5–13.

1. Enlarge Spiral Pattern 55%. Transfer pattern onto blue poster board.

2. Transfer Balloons Pattern onto assorted colored card stock. Cut two of each.
Continued on page 88.

Continued from page 87.

3. Transfer Candles Pattern onto assorted colored and yellow card stocks. Cut out seven pairs of candles.

4. Trim flame off of multicolored candles and adhere colored bases to yellow candles.

5. Transfer Gift Tag Pattern onto assorted colored card stock. Cut two.

6. Transfer Noisemaker Pattern onto hot-pink card stock. Cut two.

7. Transfer Numbers Pattern representing age of birthday onto assorted colored card stock. Cut two.

8. Transfer Gift with Ribbon Pattern onto assorted colored card stock. Cut four.

9. Transfer Splash Pattern onto assorted colored card stock. Cut two.

10. Using craft punch, punch out fifteen balloons from assorted colored card stock.

11. Cut out spiral. Embellish designs as desired.

12. Using black pen, write desired message on tag.

13. Using hole punch, punch hole in center of spiral. Cut 28" piece of ribbon. Insert ribbon through hole. Knot at one end to hold in place. Note: The ribbon will suspend the spiral from the ceiling.

14. Using push pins, pierce tiny holes in spiral to suspend designs.

15. Cut eight pieces of thread in desired lengths to hang designs from spiral.

16. Sandwich one end of thread vertically between each set of pairs. Match and adhere pairs together.

17. Insert remaining end of thread through pierced holes. Repeat for all designs. Adhere thread onto spiral with balloon punches.

New Arrival

Materials & Tools

Card stock: assorted colors; assorted patterns; blue; green; yellow

Hole punch: ¼"

Patterns: animals (pg. 121–122);9 Spiral (pg. 120); Tiny Star (pg. 122)

Pink heart stickers

Poster board: green

Push pin

White thread

Yellow satin ribbon: ¼"-wide (1 yd.)

Instructions

Refer to General Instructions on pages 5–13.

1. Enlarge Spiral Pattern 55%. Transfer pattern onto green poster board.

2. Transfer animal patterns onto assorted colored card stocks. Cut two of each.

3. Transfer Tiny Star Pattern onto yellow card stock. Cut four.

4. Cut out spiral. Embellish animals as desired.

5. Using hole punch, punch eyes in each animal. Adhere blue card stock behind eye openings of animals before matching and adhering pairs together.

6. Using hole punch, punch hole in center of spiral. Cut 28" piece of ribbon. Insert ribbon through hole. Knot at one end to hold in place. Note: The ribbon will suspend the spiral from the ceiling.

7. Using push pin, pierce tiny holes in spiral to suspend designs.

8. Cut eight pieces of thread in desired lengths to hang designs from spiral.

9. Sandwich one end of thread vertically between each set of pairs. Match and adhere pairs together.

10. Insert remaining end of thread through pierced holes. Repeat for all designs. Adhere thread onto spiral with heart stickers.

11. Place heart stickers back-to-back onto mobile threads as desired.

Mazel Tov

Materials & Tools

Card stock: gold metallic

Hole punch: ¼"

Patterns: Gift Tag (pg. 120); Spiral (pg. 120)

Poster board: blue

Push pin

Stickers: assorted Hanukkah stickers with symmetrical or mirror images; gold stars

White satin ribbon: ¼"-wide (1 yd.)

White thread

Instructions

Refer to General Instructions on pages 5–13.

1. Transfer Spiral Pattern onto blue poster board.

2. Transfer Gift Tag Pattern onto metallic card stock. Cut two.

3. Cut out spiral. Embellish gift tag with Hanukkah stickers.

4. Using hole punch, punch hole in center of spiral. Cut 28" piece of ribbon. Insert ribbon through hole. Knot at one end to hold in place. Note: The ribbon will suspend the spiral from the ceiling.

5. Sandwich one end of thread vertically between each set of stickers. Make certain stickers are symmetrical or are mirror images of each other. Match and adhere pairs together.

6. Using push pin, pierce tiny holes to suspend designs from spiral.

7. Insert remaining end of thread through pierced holes. Repeat for all designs. Adhere thread to spiral with gold star stickers.

Dangle Cards

Dangle Cards have one or more elements that are suspended so that they dangle and are visible through a window. The card can be positioned so that it reads vertically or horizontally.

Thread is sandwiched between two matching designs to create the hanging elements. A photograph can also be substituted for the design. It is important for the thread to be the same color as the background color of the card so that the shapes seem to magically suspend in midair.

Tape thread with design or photograph attached to the back of the card before adhering the cover to the card. See photograph below. Note: The cover is on the left and the card is on the right.

The card cover is free for a message or for designs themed to match the sentiments inside the card. The Dangle Card is a great vehicle for a word of encouragement ("Hang in There"); for a retirement message ("Time to Hang It Up"); or a card for anytime ("Just Hanging Around").

Just A Note

Materials & Tools

Black felt-tipped pen

Card stock: black/white polka-dot; black/white musical patterned; red; red/white polka-dot; white; yellow

Cover stock: black

Double-sided tape

Patterns: Accordion Card with Cut Out (pg. 123); Letters (pg. 125); Tiny Musical Note (pg. 122)

Press-on letters for Just A Note To Say: ¼"

Ruler

Transparent tape

Yellow thread

Instructions

Refer to General Instructions on pages 5–13.

1. Enlarge Accordion Card with Cut Out Pattern 63%. Transfer pattern onto musical patterned card stock.

2. Transfer Letters Pattern for H and I onto red/white polka-dot card stock. Repeat.

3. Transfer Tiny Musical Note onto black/white polka-dot card stock.

4. Cut out card and designs. Using craft knife, cut out window.

5. Crease card on perforation lines.

6. Cut 6¼" x 9¼" cover from cover stock. Fold in half widthwise.

7. Cut 6" x 9" lining from yellow card stock. Fold in half widthwise. Center and adhere lining to inside of cover, leaving black border all around.

8. Sandwich one end of thread vertically between each set of letters. Match and adhere letters together.

9. Tape thread to top inside opening of card so letters dangle in window. See photograph on facing page.

10. Cut 4¾" x 1½" rectangle from red card stock.

11. Using black pen and ruler, create border around inside edge of rectangle. Write desired message on rectangle.

12. Adhere rectangle onto bottom of card.

13. Cut 2" square from white card stock.

14. Using black pen and ruler, create border around inside edge of square. Adhere tiny musical note onto inside of square.

15. Cut 4½" x 3¼" rectangle from yellow card stock. Center and adhere white square onto rectangle.

16. Place letters on rectangle for Just A Note To Say.

17. Cut mat ¼" larger than rectangle all around from red card stock.

18. Adhere rectangle onto mat. Adhere mat onto front of cover.

19. Adhere one end of card ⅛" from top inside edge of cover. Repeat for remaining end of card and edge of cover.

A Thank You

Materials & Tools

Adhesive foam dots

Button: ¾" wooden heart

Card stock: assorted red patterned; denim

Cover stock: yellow/white checkered, two-sided

Craft knife

Craft punch: tiny heart

Double-sided tape

Patterns: Accordion Card with Cut Out (pg. 123); Heart #2 (pg. 122); Primitive Hearts (pg. 107)

Pens: black felt-tipped; silver metallic

Raffia scrap

Stickers: bow; tulip bouquet

Yellow thread

Instructions

Refer to General Instructions on pages 5–13.

1. Enlarge Accordion Card with Cut Out Pattern 63%. Transfer pattern onto denim card stock.

2. Transfer Heart #2 Pattern onto red patterned paper. Repeat.

3. Transfer Primitive Hearts Pattern onto red patterned card stock.

4. Cut out card and designs. Using craft knife, cut out window.

5. Crease card on perforation lines.

6. Cut 6½" x 9½" cover from cover stock. Fold in half widthwise.
Continued on page 94.

Continued from page 93.

7. Sandwich one end of thread vertically between small hearts. Match and adhere hearts together.

8. Tape thread to top inside opening of card so heart dangles in window. See photograph.

9. Using craft punch, punch out several hearts from red patterned paper. Adhere hearts around opening of card. See photograph.

10. Place bouquet sticker on bottom right of card. Place bow sticker over stems of bouquet.

11. Cut 2¼" x 1¼" rectangle from red patterned card stock.

12. Using black pen, write desired message on rectangle.

13. Cut mat ¼" larger than rectangle all around from yellow/white checkered card stock.

14. Adhere rectangle onto mat. Center and adhere mat onto top of card with foam dot.

15. Cut mat ¼" larger than primitive heart all around from red patterned card stock. Adhere primitive heart onto mat.

16. Cut 2½" x 6½" rectangle from denim card stock. Repeat. Adhere rectangles onto bottom front of card cover.

17. Center and adhere primitive heart at slight angle onto front of cover.

18. Thread raffia through button and tie in knot. Trim ends. Adhere button onto center of primitive heart.

19. Using silver pen, write desired message along right edge of primitive heart.

20. Adhere one end of card ⅛" from top inside edge of cover. Repeat for remaining end of card and edge of cover.

We're Engaged

Materials & Tools

Adhesive foam dots

Black felt-tipped pen

Card stock: cream; dk. tan; tan

Color copy of photograph

Cover stock: cream

Craft knife

Double-sided tape

Patterns: Accordion Card with Cut Out
  (pg. 123); Love (pg. 118)

Ruler

Stickers: assorted floral

Tan thread

Instructions

Refer to General Instructions on pages 5–13.

1. Enlarge Accordion Card with Cut Out Pattern 63%. Transfer pattern onto tan card stock.

2. Transfer Love Pattern onto cream card stock. Repeat.

3. Cut out card and designs. Using craft knife, cut out window.

4. Crease card on perforation lines.

5. Cut 9½" x 6½" cover from cover stock. Fold in half widthwise.

6. Sandwich one end of thread vertically between love pair. Match and adhere pair together.

Continued on page 96.

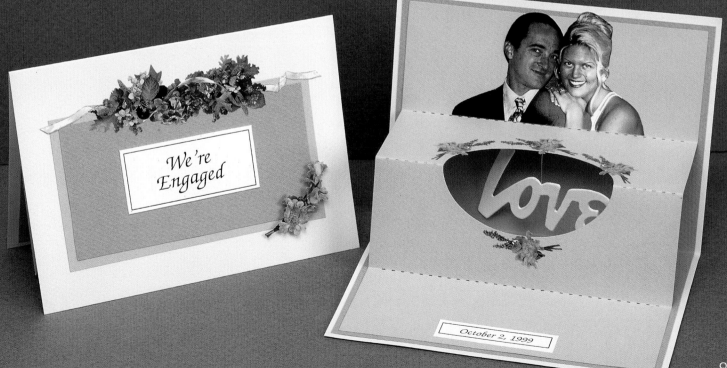

Continued from page 95.

7. Tape thread to top inside opening of card so love dangles in window. See photograph on page 95.

8. Place floral stickers around window of card as desired.

9. Cut 2¼" x ½" rectangle from cream card stock.

10. Using black pen and ruler, create border around rectangle. Write message on rectangle.

11. Center and adhere rectangle onto bottom of card.

12. Crop photograph to fit on top inside of card. Adhere photograph onto top of card.

13. Cut 9¼" x 6¼" mat from dk. tan card stock. Adhere mat onto inside of cover.

14. Cut 2¾" x 1¼" rectangle from cream card stock.

15. Using black pen and ruler, create border around rectangle. Write desired message on rectangle.

16. Cut 5" x 3¼" mat from dk. tan card stock. Center and adhere rectangle onto mat.

17. Cut second mat ¼" larger than first mat all around. Center and adhere mats together. Center and adhere mat onto front of cover.

18. Place floral sticker along top edge of mat, overlapping mat. Place foam dot on one floral sticker. Place floral sticker on bottom right edge of mat.

19. Adhere one end of card ⅛" from top inside edge of cover. Repeat for remaining end of card and edge of cover.

Working Too Hard

Materials & Tools

Adhesive foam dots

Blue thread

Card stock: black; cream; gold metallic; red; tan

Color-copied photograph and mirror image

Cover stock: blue

Double-sided tape

Patterns: Accordion Card with Cut Out (pg. 123); Clipboard (pg. 123); Pocket Watch (pg. 122)

Pens: gold metallic; white felt-tipped

Ruler

Instructions

Refer to General Instructions on pages 5–13.

1. Enlarge Accordion Card with Cut Out Pattern 63%. Transfer pattern onto tan card stock.

2. Transfer Clipboard Pattern onto onto red card stock. Repeat with black and gold card stocks.

3. Transfer Pocket Watch Pattern onto black card stock. Repeat with cream, gold, and red card stocks.

4. Cut out card and designs. Using craft knife, cut out window. Embellish clipboard and pocket watch as desired.

5. Crease card on perforation lines.

6. Assemble pocket watch and adhere onto left side of card. See photograph below.

7. Cut 9½" x 6½" cover from cover stock. Fold in half widthwise.

13. Tape thread to top inside opening of card so photograph dangles in window. See photograph below.

14. Adhere clipboard onto front of cover as desired.

8. Cut ½" x 4" rectangle from black card stock.

9. Using white pen and ruler, create border around rectangle. Write desired message on rectangle.

10. Adhere rectangle onto right edge card.

11. Crop mirror-image photograph as desired for dangling element.

12. Sandwich one end of thread vertically between photographs. Match and adhere pair together.

15. Cut 3" x ¾" strip from black card stock. Using white pen and ruler, create border around strip. Write desired message.

16. Cut mat ⅛" larger than strip all around from red card stock.

17. Center and adhere rectangle onto mat. Center and adhere mat onto bottom front of cover.

18. Adhere one end of card ⅛" from top inside edge of cover. Repeat for remaining end of card and edge of cover.

Diorama Cards

Diorama Cards provide a quick and easy way to send a three-dimensional message. The card lies flat for mailing, but converts easily to 3-D in the hands of the recipient. See photograph at right for Diorama Card after it is cut out.

Creasing on the perforation lines, and sliding the inside "card tab" through the slit, creates a simple but effective three-dimensional card with lots of room for themed decoration.

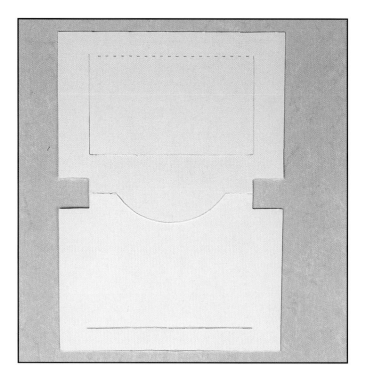

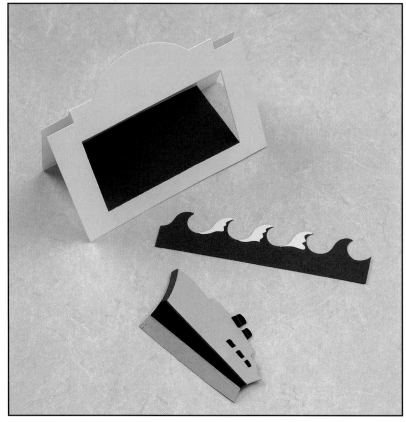

Whether the designs are attached to the card tab by a fold, or inserted through slits cut in the card tab, assembly is easy.

Create Diorama Cards for any occasion by matching the design elements to the theme of the card.

Happy Happy Birthday

Materials & Tools

Adhesive foam dots

Card stock: assorted colors; assorted patterns; black; red; white; yellow

Cover stock: black

Craft knife

Double-sided tape

Patterns: Balloon (pg. 124); Candles (pg. 106); Diorama Arch Card (pg. 124)

Pens: silver metallic; white

Ruler

Sticker strips: assorted colors

Instructions

Refer to General Instructions on pages 5–13.

1. Enlarge Diorama Arch Card Pattern 60%. Transfer pattern onto black cover stock.

2. Transfer Balloon Pattern onto assorted card stock. Repeat.

3. Transfer Candles Pattern onto assorted colored and yellow card stocks. Cut out candles.

Continued on page 100.

Continued from page 99.

4. Trim flame off of assorted colored candles and adhere onto yellow candles.

5. Cut out card. Using craft knife cut slits in card.

6. Crease card on perforation lines.

7. Cut 6¼" x 4¾" rectangle from red card stock.

8. Adhere red rectangle onto back inside of card.

9. Cut 3½" x 1¼" rectangle from black card stock.

10. Using white pen and ruler, create border around rectangle. Write desired message on rectangle.

11. Cut mat ¼" larger than black rectangle all around from white card stock.

12. Adhere rectangle onto mat. Center and adhere mat onto inside back of card.

13. Using silver pen and ruler, create border around front of card.

14. Cut strip sticker into confetti. Place confetti on front of card.

15. Place foam dot on back of one balloon. Place balloons on right top front of card, overlapping foam-dotted balloon on top.

16. Using silver pen, draw highlights on balloons. Draw balloon strings.

17. Tape candles together in groups of twos and threes. Fold candle ends under ¼". Cut three slits in card tab for candles.

18. Slip folded ends of candle groups through slits. Tape ends to back of tab, allowing candles to stand up.

19. Slip tab into card slit to assemble card.

This basic Diorama Card can be decorated for any occasion by altering the theme of the designs.

Jesse

Materials & Tools

Blue felt-tipped marker

Card stock: blue; blue/white polka-dot; dk. blue; yellow/white checkered

Cover stock: cream

Craft knife

Double-sided tape

Patterns: Baby Bootie (pg. 123); Diorama Stage Card (pg. 124)

Press-on letters for name: ¼"

Ruler

Instructions

Refer to General Instructions on pages 5–13.

1. Enlarge Diorama Stage Card Pattern 64%. Transfer pattern onto cream cover stock.

2. Transfer front section of Diorama Stage Card Pattern onto blue card stock for card border.

3. Transfer Baby Bootie Pattern onto fold of blue/white polka-dot card stock. Note: Cutting bootie on the fold creates a tab for attaching it to card. Repeat with cream card stock.

4. Transfer back of Diorama Stage Card Pattern onto yellow/white checkered card stock for lining.

5. Cut out card and designs. Embellish bootie as desired. Using craft knife, cut slits.

6. Adhere checkered lining onto inside back of card.

7. Using craft knife and ruler, cut out ½"-wide border from blue card front. See photograph.

8. Adhere blue border of card onto front of card.

9. Adhere a piece of dk. blue card stock onto back of bootie opening. Adhere laces onto bootie.

10. Tape bootie's tab onto card tab, allowing bootie to stand up.

11. Place letters on top arch of card for name.

12. Using blue marker, write birth information above card front opening.

13. Slip tab into slit to assemble card.

Bon Voyage

Materials & Tools

Adhesive foam dots

Card stock: black; blue; gold; dk. gray; gray; orange; red

Cover stock: white

Craft punch: sun

Double-sided tape

Hole punch: ⅟₁₆"

Patterns: Diorama Stage Card (pg. 124); Ocean Liner (pg. 122); Waves (pg. 124)

Press-on letters for desired message: ¼"

Instructions

Refer to General Instructions on pages 5–13.

1. Enlarge Diorama Stage Card Pattern 64%. Transfer onto white cover stock.

2. Transfer back section of Diorama Stage Card Pattern onto gold card stock.

3. Transfer Waves Pattern onto blue card stock.

4. Transfer Ocean Liner Pattern onto fold of gray card stock. Note: Cutting ocean liner on the fold, creates a tab for attaching it to card. Repeat on black; dk. gray; and red card stocks for embellishing ocean liner. Cut out designs.

5. Crease card on perforation lines. Embellish ocean liner as desired. Using craft knife, cut slits.

6. Adhere back section of card onto inside of card. Adhere a piece of blue card stock onto tab of card.

7. Cut three caps for waves from white cover stock. Adhere caps to desired waves. Adhere waves ⅛" from bottom of card.

8. Cut ⅟₁₆" border from black card stock to go around top curve of card. Adhere border around top curve.

9. Using hole punch, punch three holes at end of each border.

10. Adhere a piece of black card stock behind holes.

11. Tape ocean liner's tab onto card tab, allowing ocean liner to stand up.

12. Using craft punch, punch out sun from yellow card stock. Repeat on orange card stock. Adhere suns together, allowing orange sun to show through yellow sun.

13. Place sun onto top center of card below black border with foam dot.

14. Place letters on card for desired message.

15. Slip tab into slit to assemble card.

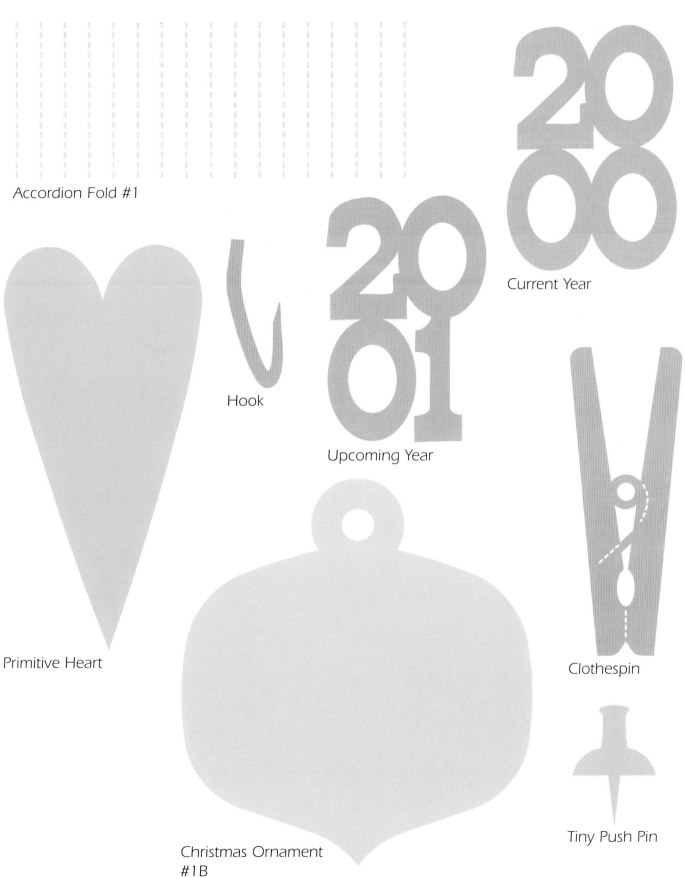

Accordion Fold #1

Current Year

Hook

Upcoming Year

Primitive Heart

Clothespin

Christmas Ornament
#1B

Tiny Push Pin

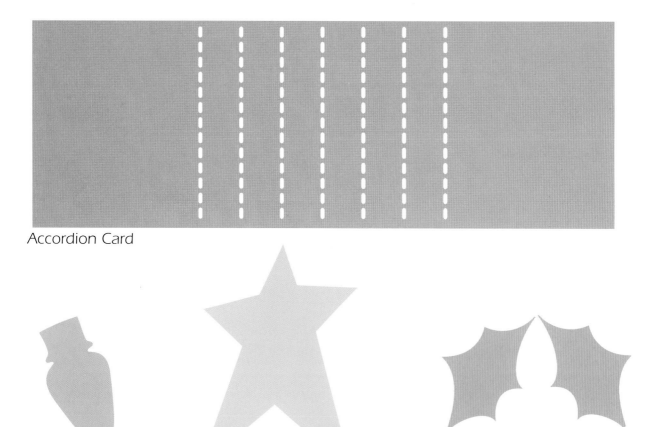

Accordion Card

Tiny Christmas Light

Primitive Star

Holly Leaves

Christmas Ornament #2A

Country Christmas Tree

104

Large Accordion Card

Accordion Fold #2

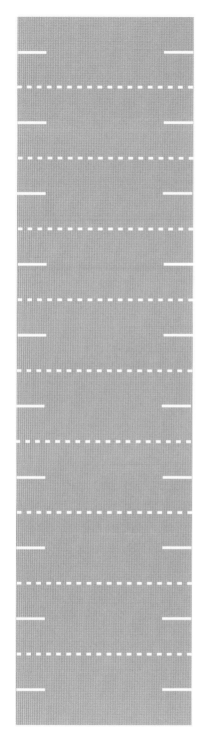

Accordion Fold with Slits

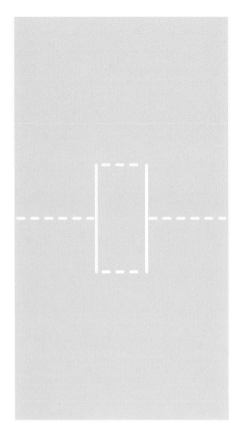

Pop-Up #1

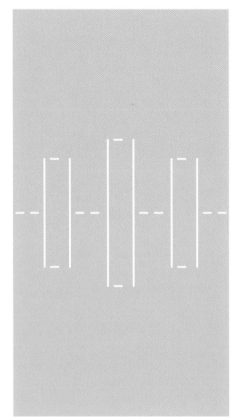

Pop-Up #3

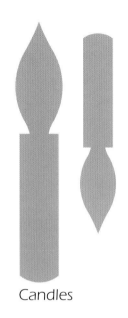

Candles

Arrow

Ghost #2

Tiny Pumpkin

0123456789

Numbers

Primitive Hearts

Small Primitive Star

Tiny Button

Carrot

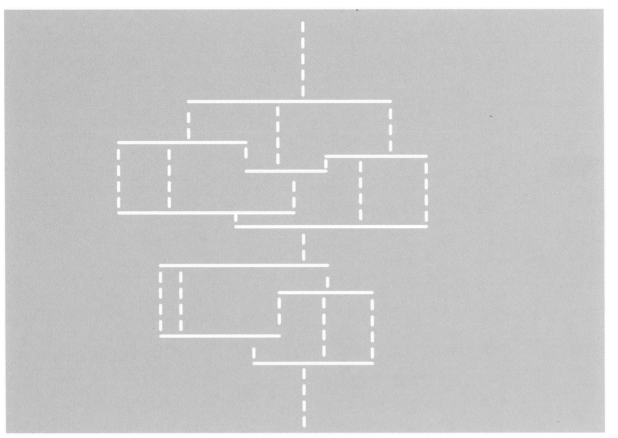

Multiple Pop-Up #1

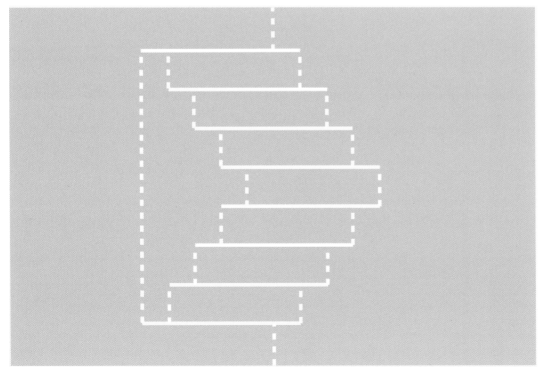

Multiple Pop-Up #2

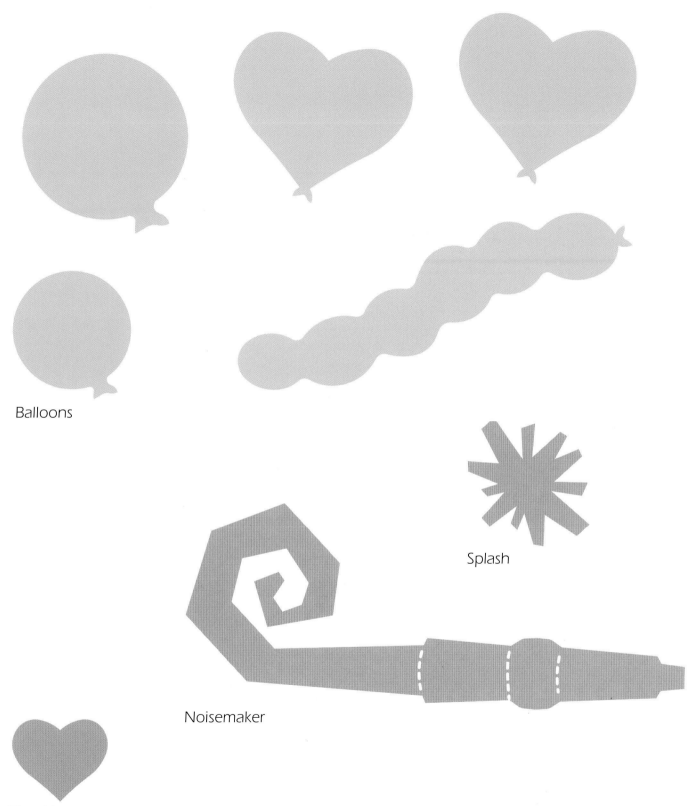

Balloons

Splash

Noisemaker

Tiny Heart

109

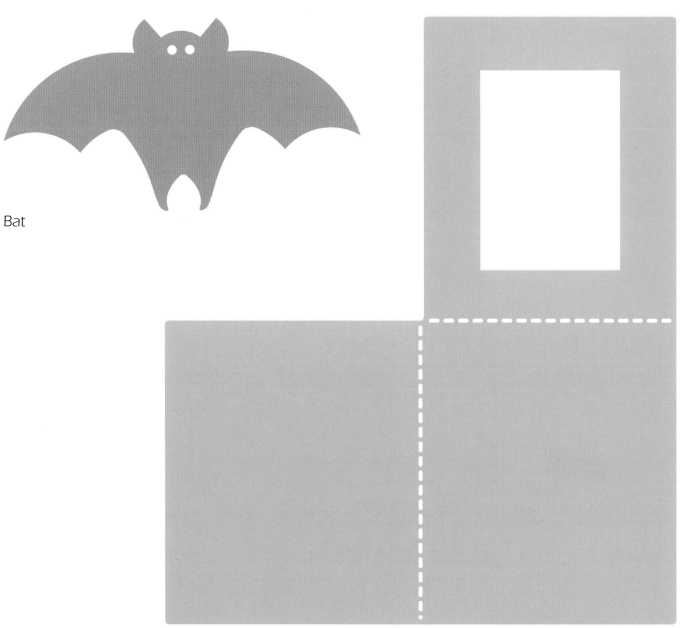

Bat

Picture Frame Fold Up Card

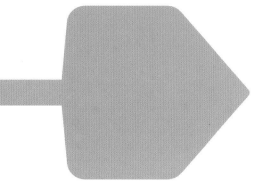

Dreidel

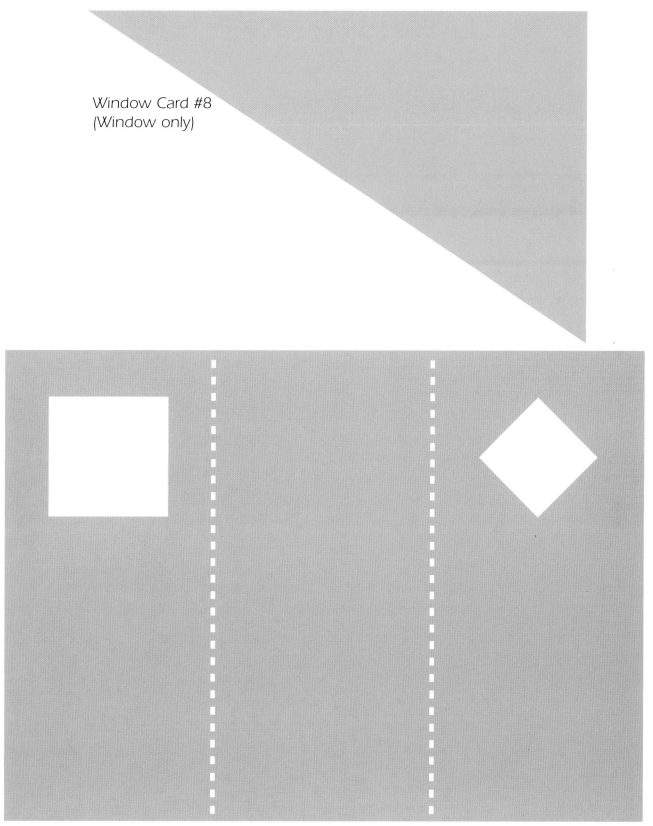

Window Card #8
(Window only)

Geometric Tri-Fold #2

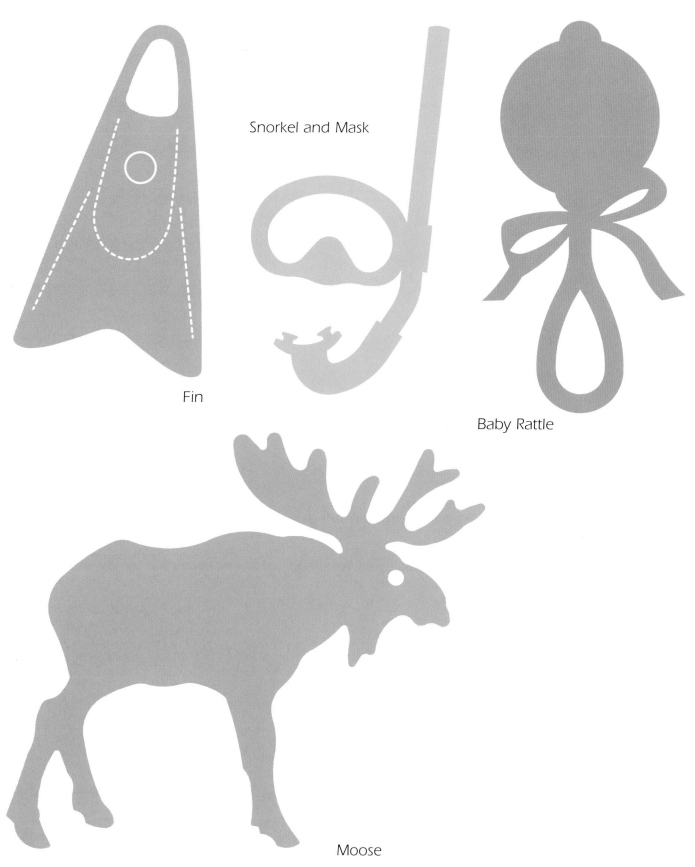

Snorkel and Mask

Fin

Baby Rattle

Moose

112

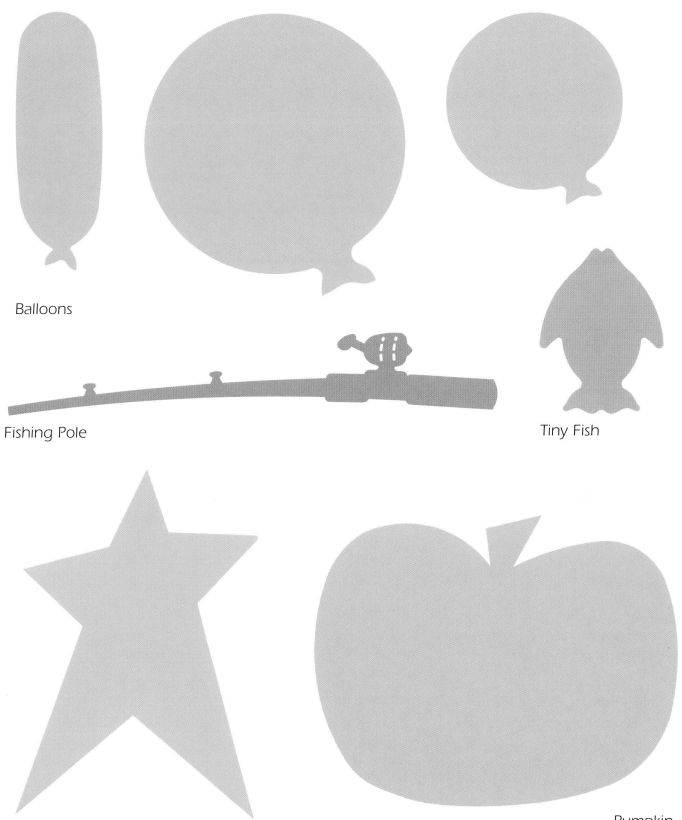

Balloons

Fishing Pole

Tiny Fish

Primitive Star

Pumpkin

Window Card #5

Smaller Puffy Star

Smaller Puffy Star Mat

Overlapping Card A

Overlapping Card B

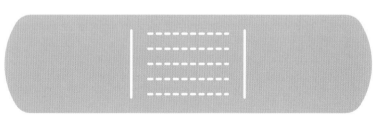

Bandage

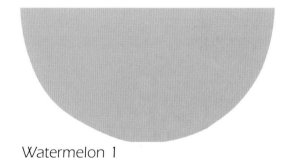

Watermelon 1

Tiny Check Mark

Watermelon 2

Envelope #3

Curved Arrow

Glass with Straws

Hand

116

Baby Booties

Larger Puffy Star

Larger Puffy Star Mat (optional)

Love

Thanks

Heart #3A

118

Envelope #2A

Small Heart

Goose

Tree Border

119

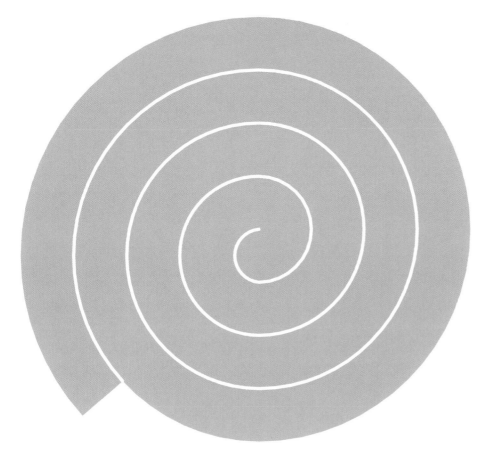

Spiral

Gift Tag

Gift with Ribbon

Heart #1A

120

Cherub

Fish #2

Duck Toy

Lamb Toy

Pig Toy

121

Chick Toy

Tiny Star

Tiny Musical Note

Rabbit #4

Heart #2

Ocean Liner

Pocket Watch

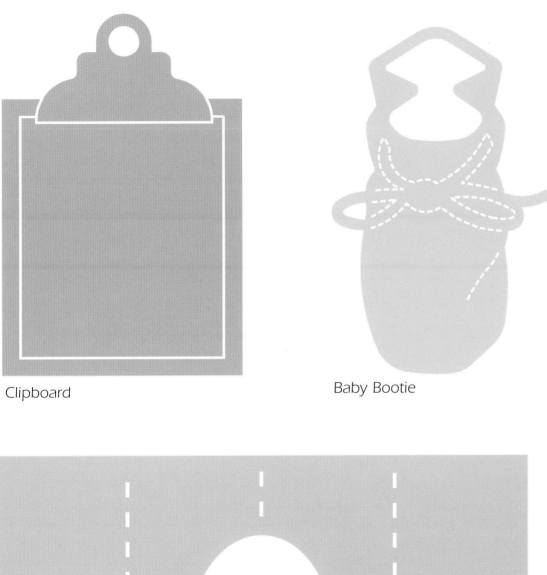

Clipboard

Baby Bootie

Accordion Card with Cut Out

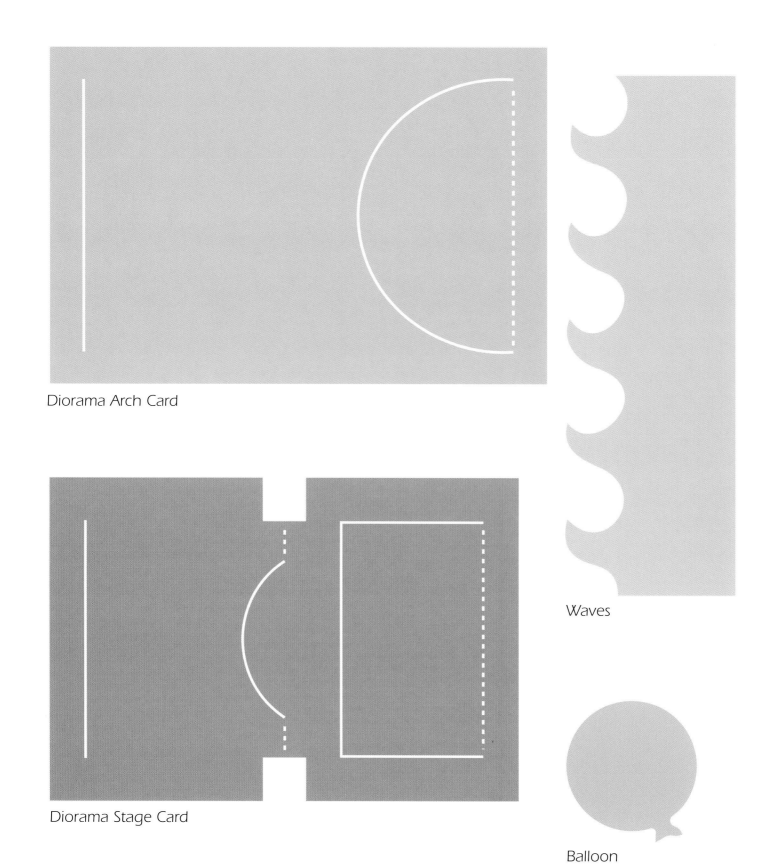

Diorama Arch Card

Waves

Diorama Stage Card

Balloon

ABCDEFGHI
JKLMNOPQ
RSTUVWXYZ
abcdefghi
jklmnopqrs
tuvwxyz;'?(!)

Lollipop Alphabet

Ellison® Dies

Name	Stock No.
Cards, Envelopes and Folds:	
Accordion Card	A102
Accordion Card With Cut Out	A103
Accordion Fold #1	A100
Accordion Fold #2	A101
Diorama Arch Card	C196
Diorama Stage Card	C197
Envelope #2A	E5002
Envelope #3	E5003
Geometric Tri-Fold #2	C192
Multiple Pop-Up #1	P800
Multiple Pop-Up #2	P799
Picture Frame Fold Up Card	P518
Pop-Up #1	P811
Pop-Up #3	P813
Window Card #5	C201
Window Card #8	C204
Decorative Dies:	
Arrow	H318
Baby Bootie	B106
Baby Booties	B107
Baby Rattle	B097
Balloons	B130, B132
Bandage	B142
Bat	B154
Candles	C156
Carrot	F790

Name	Stock No.
Cherub	C415
Chick Toy	C441
Christmas Ornament #1B	C474
Christmas Ornament #2A	C475
Clipboard	C520
Clothespin	C538
Country Christmas Tree	C488
Curved Arrow	A801
Dreidel	D670
Duck Toy	D891
Fin	S992
Fish #2	F482
Fishing Pole	F491
Ghost #2	G451
Gift Tag	T145
Gift with Ribbon	G454
Glass with Straws	G509
Goose	G660
Hand	C446
Heart #1A	H315
Heart #2	H312
Heart #3A	H313
Holly Leaves	H770
Lamb Toy	L101
Large Puffy Star	S814
Lollipop Alphabet	
(lower case)	2"
(upper case)	4"
Love	W923
Moose	M703

Name	Stock No.
Noisemaker (Party Noisemaker #2)	P176
Ocean Liner	D120
Pig Toy	P533
Pocket Watch	W156
Primitive Heart	H316
Primitive Hearts	H316
Primitive Star	S817
Pumpkin	P900
Puffy Star Mat	S809
Rabbit #4	R102
Small Primitive Star	S818
Small Puffy Star	S814
Snorkel and Mask	S457
Spiral	S760
Splash	P176
Thanks	W910
Tiny Balloons	B131
Tiny Button	B982
Tiny Check Mark	C405
Tiny Christmas Light	C481
Tiny Fish	F483
Tiny Heart	H310, H320
Tiny Musical Note	M902
Tiny Pumpkin	B770TU
Tiny Push Pin	P941
Tiny Star	S812
Tree Border	B770TR
Watermelon1	W160
Watermelon 2	W160
Waves	D56013

Metric Conversion Chart

mm-millimetres   cm-centimetres
inches to millimetres and centimetres

inches	mm	cm	inches	cm	inches	cm
⅛	3	0.3	9	22.9	30	76.2
¼	6	0.6	10	25.4	31	78.7
⅜	10	1.0	11	27.9	32	81.3
½	13	1.3	12	30.5	33	83.8
⅝	16	1.6	13	33.0	34	86.4
¾	19	1.9	14	35.6	35	88.9
⅞	22	2.2	15	38.1	36	91.4
1	25	2.5	16	40.6	37	94.0
1¼	32	3.2	17	43.2	38	96.5
1½	38	3.8	18	45.7	39	99.1
1¾	44	4.4	19	48.3	40	101.6
2	51	5.1	20	50.8	41	104.1
2½	64	6.4	21	53.3	42	106.7
3	76	7.6	22	55.9	43	109.2
3½	89	8.9	23	58.4	44	111.8
4	102	10.2	24	61.0	45	114.3
4½	114	11.4	25	63.5	46	116.8
5	127	12.7	26	66.0	47	119.4
6	152	15.2	27	68.6	48	121.9
7	178	17.8	28	71.1	49	124.5
8	203	20.3	29	73.7	50	127.0

yards to metres

yards	metres	yards	metres	yards	metres	yards	metres	yards	metres
⅛	0.11	2⅛	1.94	4⅛	3.77	6⅛	5.60	8⅛	7.43
¼	0.23	2¼	2.06	4¼	3.89	6¼	5.72	8¼	7.54
⅜	0.34	2⅜	2.17	4⅜	4.00	6⅜	5.83	8⅜	7.66
½	0.46	2½	2.29	4½	4.11	6½	5.94	8½	7.77
⅝	0.57	2⅝	2.40	4⅝	4.23	6⅝	6.06	8⅝	7.89
¾	0.69	2¾	2.51	4¾	4.34	6¾	6.17	8¾	8.00
⅞	0.80	2⅞	2.63	4⅞	4.46	6⅞	6.29	8⅞	8.12
1	0.91	3	2.74	5	4.57	7	6.40	9	8.23
1⅛	1.03	3⅛	2.86	5⅛	4.69	7⅛	6.52	9⅛	8.34
1¼	1.14	3¼	2.97	5¼	4.80	7¼	6.63	9¼	8.46
1⅜	1.26	3⅜	3.09	5⅜	4.91	7⅜	6.74	9⅜	8.57
1½	1.37	3½	3.20	5½	5.03	7½	6.86	9½	8.69
1⅝	1.49	3⅝	3.31	5⅝	5.14	7⅝	6.97	9⅝	8.80
1¾	1.60	3¾	3.43	5¾	5.26	7¾	7.09	9¾	8.92
1⅞	1.71	3⅞	3.54	5⅞	5.37	7⅞	7.20	9⅞	9.03
2	1.83	4	3.66	6	5.49	8	7.32	10	9.14

Index